ABSOLUTELY FRANK

Bryan Hennessey

ABSOLUTELY FRANK

Bryan Hennessey

Killick Press
an imprint of Creative Publishers
St. John's, Newfoundland
1997

The Canada Council for the Arts since 1957 | Le Conseil des Arts du Canada depuis 1957

We acknowledge the support of the Canada Council for the Arts for our publishing program

∝ Printed on acid-free paper

Cover design: Shelley Cornick

Published by
KILLICK PRESS
a Creative Book Publishing imprint
A Robinson-Blackmore Printing & Publishing associated company
P.O. Box 8660, St. John's, Newfoundland A1B 3T7

Printed in Canada by:
ROBINSON-BLACKMORE PRINTING & PUBLISHING

Canadian Cataloguing in Publication Data

Hennessey, Bryan, 1949-

Absolutely Frank
ISBN 1-895387-88-4

I. Title. II. Weekend A.M. (Radio program).

PS8565.E584A73 1997 C812'.54 C97-950219-5
PR9199.3.H4523A73 1997

*This book is dedicated to several different people,
for several different reasons: to my brother Jay,
who introduced me to The Goon Show and Mad Magazine
when I was a child; to Jamie, Ingrid and Suzanne
for their support and enthusiasm; to Richard Beaton,
who always had an encouraging word;
to my wife and daughter, who had to
put up with me during my masquerade as "Frank";
and to everyone who listened and enjoyed.*

CONTENTS

PREFACE

For a little over three years, from May 1993 to November 1996, I had the happy task of writing and performing a bi-weekly feature for CBC Radio's Saturday morning Arts Programme, Week-End A. M. During that time, I plagued the airwaves under the *nom de radio* of "Absolutely Frank."

As with so many things that have happened in my life and (for want of a better word) career, the character of Absolutely Frank came into existence in a random, almost accidental, manner.

During the provincial election campaign in the Spring of 1993, I got a phone call from Suzanne Woolridge of CBC Radio. She asked me if I could do a brief commentary on the election.

As I am nothing if not opinionated on almost any subject, I figured I could probably throw together a five-minute gripe about our local politics and politicians. I then asked Suzanne the only really important question: how much does it pay? She named a figure. I said "Uh huh" and then she added that the gig paid a bit more if I were to create a "character" who would deliver my diatribe, rather than simply appearing as myself.

Without thinking, I blurted that I did indeed have a "character" to do my talking for me. Suzanne asked me his name. I said the first thing that came into my head: "Oh, he's called 'Absolutely Frank,' and he's outraged by everything."

Thus, from a combination of greed and necessity, Absolutely Frank was born.

Having invented him, I was then faced with the problem of trying to figure out who he was. Over the next few months, as I did more commentaries, Frank began to emerge more clearly in my mind.

However he came across to the listening public, to me Frank was the Voice of the Ordinary, if slightly peeved, Citizen, simultaneously disgusted and amused by the wide range of human folly. Frank was especially irked by politicians. They are, admittedly, an easy target, particularly in Newfoundland, which seems to grow a uniquely dense and dunderheaded breed.

But as you will see from the variety of topics in this collection, just about everything got on Frank's nerves. From televised sports to tobacco taxes, from cults to pop culture: you name it, Frank was bugged by it. How he avoided a burst blood vessel or an attack of spontaneous combustion is beyond me.

A few people have asked: how much of Frank was me and vice versa? That's difficult to say. I'm a much more serene person than Frank. I'm quite content as long as I've got food in the fridge, a book to read and Cable TV. On the other hand, I share with Frank a sense of outrage at the many absurdities that confront us as we lurch towards the Millennium. The major difference between Frank and me is that I don't have an obnoxious Cousin Ted driving me batty all the time.

To answer another often-asked question: Cousin Ted was not based on anybody I knew personally (thank God). Ted appeared spontaneously in an early commentary merely to illustrate a point Frank was making at the time, and he quickly took on a loathsome life of his own.

When I began compiling this collection, I noticed two things: the commentaries themselves gradually evolved from simple "opinion" pieces into what amounted to little five-minute radio plays. I'm not sure how this happened, but I think it made the Franks more interesting; certainly, they became more interesting to write and perform.

The other thing I noticed was how Frank's wife Hazel began to emerge as a major character. I was aided in this process by CBC Radio producer Francesca Swann (thanks, Francesca!), who graciously consented to become the Voice of Hazel. I was able to do the voices for Frank and Cousin Ted myself, but I needed someone to be Hazel for me; specifically, someone who wasn't a recognizable CBC Radio "voice." The fact that

Francesca is English proved to be an unexpected bonus: who would have thought that Frank, that quintessential townie, had an English wife?

My personal thanks are extended to Suzanne Woolridge for her original phone call, without which Frank would never have existed, and to my two radio producers, Ingrid Fraser and Jamie Fitzpatrick. Their always-constructive criticisms were most helpful in shaping Frank's personality and viewpoint.

Thanks as well to Ed Kavanagh, Don Morgan and everyone at *The Killick Press* for believing that this was a good idea.

Finally, I owe a double thank-you to Jamie Fitzpatrick for his additional work as Editorial Consultant on this book. He gave me some valuable insights, and this is a better piece of work than it might have been without his contributions.

Bryan Hennessey
St John's, Nfld.
1997

AUTHOR'S NOTE

The astute reader will notice almost at once that these commentaries, especially as they evolved into little mini-plays, were written as radio scripts, and I've retained that format, including sound effects and music cues. I've also kept the sign-off line "For Week-End A.M., I'm Absolutely Frank" and its many variations, since the sign-off often reflected what had preceded it.

Separating the scripts into four distinct sections was Jamie's idea (using The Beatles' song titles was mine), and I happily agreed with him when I recognized the pseudo-Viconian aptness of such a framework.

(Just kidding, Joyceans!)

—B.H.

PART ONE

In My Life

Frank springs, half-formed, from the brow of Zeus and immediately begins to gripe about politics, Hollywood, televised sports and sundry other matters; Cousin Ted begins to emerge from the shadows; Frank struggles to find his own identity.

Election and Economy

This was my first "Frank," and the major issue at the time was the Newfoundland provincial election. A minor issue was the upcoming federal election. Kim Campbell had recently replaced Brian Mulroney as leader of the Progressive Conservative Party, and thus as Prime Minister. Clyde Wells was, of course, Premier of Newfoundland. Len Simms was the provincial P.C. leader. Fraser March was a powerful union leader whose large salary provoked much comment. He was also an NDP candidate in an ill-advised bid for public office.

I was just beginning to work out who Frank was and what he stood for. The scenarios and supporting cast that would emerge in the months to come were not even dreamed of at this point. In retrospect, however, Frank's roots are here, showing clearly.

Let me make it perfectly clear that I'm no economist. I don't know anything about money. I can't pay my Income Tax. I can't even balance my own cheque book.

Basically, I'm just another unemployed Newfoundlander, but I do know this much: we are in serious trouble here, and I don't know how to solve our problems any more than any other bewildered Newfoundlander does.

It's pointless to blame Clyde Wells and the Liberals, though. Liberals, Tories, NDP—what's the difference? The problems we face in Newfoundland are going to be the same no matter which crowd of boneheads plunk their fat hams down on all that nice new furniture in the Confederation Building.

Every election we hear the same stale old rhetoric, each party accusing the other of incompetence and loudly proclaiming its own, infinitely superior, programme. Well, that's nothing but politics, and what is politics, after all, but the art of managing people—thus, the art of manipulating people—thus, the art of deceiving people?

I'm often reminded of the saying: "People generally get the government they deserve." Does Newfoundland deserve the likes of condescending Clyde or the loutish Len Simms or, God help us, Fraser March, the $100,000 a year Man of the People? Does Canada deserve tired old political retreads like Jean Chretien or the starched and schoolmarmy Kim Campbell? Maybe we do, since we keep electing drones like them every four or five years.

I think what depresses me most about our political excuse-the-expression "leaders" is how damn dull they all are. They don't appear to have personalities. Did everyone get one of Clyde's Christmas cards, with Mr and Mrs Clyde and the grandchildren and the family dog? The dog looked like the only one of 'em with a personality! Maybe we ought to vote for the dog and elect a kind of crackie government. Would it make much difference? I know I, for one, would find it easier to relate to a bunch of barking dogs than I can to a pack of lawyers and businessmen.

I know that money makes the world go 'round, but I honestly don't believe you can run a country like a business. With all these dorks, it's all bottom lines and balance sheets: they like the ledgers to look tidy. But a country is, first and last, its people, and you can't run people like a business—they're just not built that way. Any government that puts balance sheets ahead of people is a government of the rich, by the rich and for the rich. Is this democracy? I prefer to think of it as "The Illusion of Democracy."

Like I said, I don't know anything about economics or politics, but I know this: whatever happens, whichever bunch of yamyucks gets itself elected, the poor and the powerless will get screwed again, and there's nothing new about that.

Pete Townshend of The Who put politics into perspective for me about twenty years ago. He wrote "Meet the New Boss, same as the Old Boss." The song was called, with succinct cynicism, *Won't Get Fooled Again*. Unfortunately, we go on fooling ourselves every election.

I do have a suggestion for saving some money, however: why don't all the MPs and MHAs from here to B.C. go off salary for a year? Donate their services for the public good and give the rest of us some incentive, some reason to believe anything they say.

I know that when they tell the rest of us to "tighten our belts" and "make sacrifices," I'd like to see the smug smiles wiped off their bloated kissers for a while—and I doubt if I'm alone in that desire.

I haven't decided yet who, if anyone, I'm going to vote for, but watching this election campaign, and thinking about politics in general, I'm reminded of another saying: "Don't vote, it only encourages them."

For Week-End A. M., I'm Absolutely Frank.

May 1993

Our Paulie

This is an uncharacteristically wistful reminiscence from Frank. It's interesting to see, however, that an excitable young Beatlemaniac still lives deep within the middle-aged crank.

Paul McCartney, former Beatle and zillionaire, is on tour again, and, though I won't get to see him perform unless I win some kind of contest, I wish him well. A while ago I happened to catch Paul's 1990 *Get Back Concert Tour* on TV. His repertoire these days includes a generous helping of songs he wrote, recorded and performed with The Beatles all those years ago.

Commercial nostalgia? Maybe. Paul was always the most commercial-minded of The Beatles, and with good reason. He has a knack for making a memorable melody, and if his lyrics are less than inspiring since his Beatle heyday—well, what the hell. Meaningful lyrics don't necessarily ensure rock & roll greatness. In Little Richard's classic *Tutti Frutti*, for instance, the words "Awopbopalobopalopbamboom!" said more about the joyful ecstasy of rock & roll than anything, say, The Who's Pete Townshend ever wrote.

No, Paul was never a lyrical heavyweight. In his prime as a Beatle he had John Lennon's more adventurous sensibilities to balance his own tendency towards what one critic accurately described as "hummable fluff." He has remained content since The Beatles' break-up to churn out scads of silly love songs, and we really shouldn't expect more of him. After all, didn't he produce with The Beatles more than enough classic 60s rock & roll to last a lifetime?

And yet . . . and yet . . .

One can't help wondering sometimes why he squanders his enormous talents on "hummable fluff." He's a fine musician and possesses one of the most extraordinary and versatile voices in the history of rock & roll. True, he produced his best and most lasting work in his 20s with The Beatles. With his first post-Beatles band, the wimpy Wings, he stubbornly avoided for several years performing any of his Beatle hits. But let's face it, if you shell out your hard-earned bucks for a Paul McCartney concert, you want him to do some of those great songs—and now he does.

And it's a pleasure to hear them being done by the man who wrote them. We've heard them done, usually badly, by billions of bar bands for years and we tend to forget just how good they really are, familiarity breeding its usual dose of contempt.

The best of them—probably the best song he ever wrote and arguably one of the best songs ever written—is *Hey Jude.*

Hey Jude evokes a potent combination of emotions. First, a wistful nostalgia for The Beatles themselves and what they meant to those of us who grew up with them; and second, an equally wistful nostalgia for our own younger selves as we stood on the brink of adulthood and all the trials and tribulations thereof.

Hey Jude captures a bittersweet moment in time and in our lives, when things didn't seem quite as bleak and purposeless as they would sometimes later appear. There was still a sense of hope, a feeling that maybe we *can* work it out.

And when good ol' Paulie bats his eyes and sings *Hey Jude,* he takes us back to that moment in time. Are we to weep for what we've lost or for what we've gained?

Mind you, I'm not one to wallow in nostalgia for the 60s. It was an interesting time, to be sure, but hardly the Groovy Golden Age of Love and Peace it's often falsely remembered as. But hearing Paul sing *Hey Jude* almost makes me believe in the possibility of something better.

Maybe that's what Paul's purpose in life is. He certainly doesn't need the money. So maybe he goes out on tour every couple of years to remind us of something we may have lost forever: innocence, optimism, our lost youth, a time when we believed, however briefly or even foolishly, that we *could* take a sad song and make it better.

One of the most remarkable—and unprecedented—things about The Beatles, after all, was how they got better and better with each new record, with each new song. And maybe that's what we now mourn and celebrate: the feeling, inspired by The Beatles, that we, too (despite tons of evidence to the contrary), could get better and better.

For Week-End A. M., I'm Absolutely Frank.

June 1993

Smokin'!

Frank's horrible Cousin Ted made his first appearance here, quite by accident. Once I'd invented him, I realized he made a very convenient scapegoat whom I could use to illustrate a variety of opinions and attitudes that send Frank into a frenzy.

Okay, I admit it: I'm a smoker. I know it's bad for me, I know it's not politically correct, but I do it anyway. I do it because I enjoy it. I don't force anyone else to do it. I prefer not to tell other people what they should or shouldn't do. It's none of my business.

Now, if some people don't want me to smoke around them, that's fine with me. That's their right, their choice. And that's really what we're talking about here—freedom of choice. Maybe you've heard of it.

Alcohol and drug abuse are killing millions of people every year, but hey—I can't make them stop doing it. People do what they do.

Take my Cousin Ted, for example. He's a Health Care nightmare—he smokes, he drinks, he pops pills, he eats nothing but fried grease. It's a miracle he's alive at all. He thinks the Canada Food Guide is a sinister Orwellian plot. And for all I know, he could be right.

But listen—you can't legislate health. You can't *force* people like Ted to be healthy. And that's exactly what the Canadian Government wants to do. It's the same kind of smug self-righteousness that brought Prohibition to the United States seventy years ago, and look what the results were: criminals got rich and people drank anyway.

The Canadian Government, God bless its Puritan heart, seems to have fallen into the same trap. Prohibition of tobacco is its ultimate goal, and history has clearly shown us that Prohibition simply doesn't work.

There's a lot of talk lately about the "Underground Economy," specifically as it relates to tobacco smuggling. Hasn't it ever occurred to the minions of the Department of Health and Welfare *why* there's a flourishing illegal tobacco trade? Because people are being forced into it by their own government!

I mean, even a nimrod like Cousin Ted has the right to choose for himself. And if Ted wants to blow his disability cheque on illegal tobacco, that's *his* problem.

Ted might be a jackass, but he's not stupid, y'know? He knows smoking is bad for him. But this endless escalation of tobacco taxes and forcing people to stand out in the freezing cold to have a smoke is just plain dumb. I mean, where are we, Nazi Germany? Are smokers going to be required to wear an identifying badge next, a yellow cigarette stitched to their jackets?

I can't help wondering if the Canadian Government really spends as much time, energy (and public money) on fighting alcohol and drug abuse as it does on warning us about the evils of tobacco. Booze and drugs do a lot more to destroy people's lives, their homes and families, the very fabric of our society; yet I don't notice crowds of drinkers being made to stand out in the cold to have a beer.

I have to support the idea of a legal age limit for buying tobacco. Smoking and drinking are an adult's choice, after all, and if adults (even amateur adults like Cousin Ted) choose to smoke and drink, that's *their* business.

Okay, okay—we'd all be better off if we didn't smoke, but I repeat: you can't legislate health. Smarmy politicians tell us again and again that we live in the Free World. If that's true, aren't we all entitled to some basic personal freedoms? Or are we only entitled to the degree of freedom that the government says is good for us?

Make no mistake—democracy or not, only the rich and powerful are truly free. The rest of us are only as free as our government allows us to be. And as Cousin Ted is fond of saying, if that's democracy, then I'm a purple-arsed baboon.

Now, if you'll excuse me, I'm going to step outside and have a smoke, before the Tobacco Gestapo bursts in here to search and beat me.

For Week-End A. M., I'm Absolutely Frank.

June 1993

The Psycho Next Door

I am *not* insane!

Some of my in-laws have occasionally called me a crackpot, but I think they were only fooling. In any case, when they call me "certifiable," I am quick to respond that insanity is not a medical term. It's a legal term, as many psychiatrists have pointed out, usually while testifying for the defense of some murderous madman.

Be that as it may, we all have a general idea of what the word means: *loco, non compos mentis,* mad as a hatter, crazy as a bag of hammers, nutty as a five-dollar fruitcake . . .

There can't be many of us who haven't known or met the odd nut-case in our lives.

Consider my Cousin Ted, for instance. When Ted goes home after one of his mercifully rare visits, I go around the house checking the carpets for teeth-marks. Most people assume Ted is more or less normal, but they don't know him like I do. In the wacky world of marginal mentalities, Ted is the King of the Macadamian Nut-Cases.

Of course, we don't call them "nut-cases" anymore. We call them "personality disorders" now. And let's face it, most of us, if the truth were known, suffer from *some* kind of personality disorder; but we learn to deal with it so we can function in the so-called "real world." We obey the laws, we observe the social and moral codes, etc. In other words, we act "normal."

(If you're listening, Ted, none of this applies to you.)

But what about the *lethal* personality disorders? What about the real criminal psychopaths? Let me give you a classic example . . .

In 1924, Nathan Leopold and Richard Loeb, the brilliant teen-age sons of wealthy and respectable Chicago families, kidnapped and murdered 14-year-old Bobby Franks, a neighbour of theirs. Their professed motive? To commit a perfect crime, baffle the authorities and demonstrate their moral and intellectual superiority over conventional society. (The fact that they left a trail of clues a mile long demonstrated the exact opposite.)

As it happened, Richard Loeb, considered by everyone to be the more "normal" one, turned out to have all the symptoms of what we would now call a psychopathic personality. A compulsive liar and thief, he had, since childhood, indulged in petty crimes and misdemeanors, depending on his boyish charm and his influential family to save his skin time after time. Unlike Leopold, he displayed no remorse for any of his crimes. Indeed, he didn't seem to comprehend the very concept of remorse. He was, in short, a true psychopath.

So how do you recognize a psychopath?

That's the problem—you usually can't, until it's too late. Basically, your typical psychopath is just like you and me—only worse!

I mean, look at Cousin Ted. Aside from some revolting personal habits, he's as outwardly normal as anyone else. As far as I know, he's never murdered anyone or committed any major crimes. The closest he's ever come to stripping away the Mask of Sanity and revealing his true psycho self was when he got caught drunk-driving his mother's stolen car inside the Avalon Mall. And then he had the colossal gall to insist he was raffling it off for the Head Injury Society! Well, you may have fooled everyone else, Ted, but you don't fool me!

Of course, the average psychopath (if there is such a thing), isn't usually a murderer anyway. More commonly, he's merely a habitual petty criminal or monumental screw-up like Ted. Even more commonly, he scuttles his way through life using and manipulating other people, lying, cheating, making stupidly transparent excuses for his behaviour, talking his way out of trouble and glossing everything over with a glib charm that's almost plausible.

Y'know ... if that description of the average psychopath sounds like a description of the average politician ... maybe there's a finer line between madness and sanity than we think.

For Week-End A. M., I'm Absolutely Frank.

July 1993

Hair Today

No explanation necessary, except that "Lukey's Boat" was a popular and influential "heavy" rock band of the late 60s/early 70s in St. John's, led by the late Noel Dinn of "Figgy Duff" fame.

Picture it: St. John's, the summer of 1969 . . . me and my Cousin Ted are truckin' along the Water Street Mall in our bell-bottom Levis and our tie-dyed T shirts, and our hair . . . well, our hair is down to our shoulders and we're waving our freak flags high! Corner boys and pinky-drinking derelicts are shouting, "Get a haircut, ya fruits!", but me and Ted, we don't give a damn. We walk on by, heading up to Acid Road and the Free School, and the Revolution is just around the corner of McMurdo's Lane.

Far out, man.

Long hair really meant something in those days. It was, no kidding, a major social and cultural statement. Wow. Only a few years earlier, if you had anything except the standard short-back-and-sides, you would have been branded a pervert or, worse yet, an "artist."

Then came The Beatles . . . and the cosmos trembled!

When they appeared on the Ed Sullivan Show in February of '64, we saw all that hair and thought: "All right! Shag the barber! Shag the school dress code! Shag Mom and Dad! I'm growin' my hair!"

By the end of the 60s, long hair was everywhere. Even the old fogies of the day got into the act, and long (or at least longer) hair sprouted up on all sorts of unlikely heads. Take a look at some newsreel footage from back then and see what gay blades like Frank Moores and John Crosbie looked like: hair spilling over their ears and wide collars and, most amusing, the big pointy Elvis sideburns the boyos were sporting. As hilarious as they look to us now, at the time Frankie and Johnny were simply reflecting the fashion of the day. Just imagine our blue-eyed boy Clyde Wells going around with a Mohawk and a gold earring, or Little Kimmy Campbell shaving the sides of her fluffy little head, and you'll get the idea.

In the 70s, hair styles became . . . ah, forget it. The less said about the 70s, the better. Take one look at a picture of The Bee Gees in their disco heyday, with the blow-dried bouffants and the chains and medallions, and say hello to a week's worth of nightmares.

Throughout the 80s and up to the present, I'm happy to say, you can do whatever you want to with your hair. More recent trends, like half-shaved butch cuts on young girls, seem impossibly ugly to me, but, when all is said and done, who really cares? It's only hair, after all. Taking your hair too seriously is the exclusive province of the young and the pathologically vain.

Time has passed some people by, however. Cousin Ted, now an overweight, balding man in his 40s, still insists on wearing what's left of his hair in a long, greasy ponytail. "Ted," I say to him, "wake up and smell the Decaff! It ain't 1969 anymore! Lukey's Boat ain't playing at Buckmaster's Circle! The Revolution is over, ya big goof!"

Ted, of course, ignores me, lights up a joint, puts on the first King Crimson album, and goes back to giggling over his collection of Fabulous Furry Freak Brothers comic books.

Far out, Ted.

In my own case, genetics played a more decisive role than fashion. I lost most of my glossy and luxuriant locks some years ago, and I am now one of the follicly challenged. I still feel the odd twinge of regret that I no longer have as many tonsorial options as I once did, but what the heck? With the world going to hell in a handbag, and our own province engaged in a life and death struggle for survival, what we do with our hair doesn't seem to matter all that much.

My advice? Enjoy your hair while you still can, folks, before you have to tear it out in frustration.

For Week-End A. M., I'm Absolutely Balding Frank.

August 1993

Remaking Reality

Stranger-Than-Fiction Department: I recently heard rumours that Kevin Costner is planning a remake of Casablanca, *with himself in Bogie's role. Is nothing sacred?*

Oddly enough, my prediction about CBC TV's Street Legal *and* Road to Avonlea *eventually came true, proof that prayer works.*

One night, a while ago, I'm having a quiet evening at home, watching a PBS special about marsupials, when who shows up at the door but my Cousin Ted, armed with a six-pack and an Extra-Large Pizza. Yipes! The wife, the kids and the cat all hide upstairs while Ted plops himself down on the couch and starts flipping around the channels. He finally settles on yet another remake of that old neo-Gothic chestnut *Phantom of the Opera,* which has been remade at least half a dozen times, not to mention its latest incarnation as a musical by the massively untalented Andrew Lloyd Webber. Conversation with Ted being out of the question, I start thinking about . . . remakes.

The remake is a Hollywood tradition as old as Hollywood itself. The theory behind it goes something like this: if a movie did "Boffo Box" once, there's no reason why it shouldn't do "Boffo Box" again. Just hire a hot new cast, throw in all the sex and violence you couldn't show before and . . . bingo! You've got a hit! Boffo Box!

It seems like every other movie that gets made these days is a remake of some *other* movie. I suspect that there are now almost as many remakes as there are original movies. We may eventually reach the point where there are *more* remakes than originals. There is a mathematical term for this kind of logically absurd progression, but I forget what it is.

Where will it end? Will some Hollywood bonehead decide to remake *Casablanca* with Micky Rourke and Sharon Stone? Or how about Tom Cruise (and his wife) in a remake of *Citizen Kane?* Gaaaaaaah!

Or will the remake frenzy finally catch up with itself? Will Hollywood start doing remakes of movies it's just made? Maybe next year we'll have a remake of *Basic Instinct* as a musical comedy, starring Kirstie Alley, John Travolta and a talking dog.

It's really too bad we can't apply the remake principle to our own reality. We could remake the year 1963, for instance, and change the script ever-so-slightly, so Oswald survives and names all the names. Or, closer to home, we could remake the Mulroney years and hire a better actor to play Brian, someone believable . . . like, say, Wilford Brimley, the guy who does the Quaker Oats commercials. He'd make a much more convincing Mulroney than the second-rate ham we actually had. Or how about 1992? We could remake the fishery crisis and have all those bloody foreign trawlers voluntarily go home out of it . . . and, hey! They could find a way to save the whales while they're at it! Boffo Box!

If only, if only . . .

If I could do a remake of my own life, I'd probably make myself rich and famous instead of poor and obscure. I'd give myself a full head of hair and a thriving career as a best-selling novelist.

Or maybe I'd make myself the head of the CBC and cancel *Street Legal* and *Road to Avonlea* . . . forever!

At the very least, I'd remake the Night of the Living Ted. I'd give him a full-time job and a big-screen TV and get him the hell off my couch. Or . . . maybe I'd remake Ted himself . . . as an ashtray, or a carburetor. Something useful.

For Week-End A. M., I'm Absolutely Frank.

October 1993

Darkness at Noon, Death in the Afternoon

On the 30th Anniversary of the Kennedy Assassination, I simply couldn't resist putting in my two cents' worth. This is Frank in one of his more reflective moods.

I was fourteen years old. I was in school, Grade Nine, at Brother Rice. It was around three o'clock on an ordinary, boring Friday afternoon, and all we were thinking of was the freedom of the coming week-end. The principal, Billy Bellows, came on the P. A. system and gave us the news. He asked us to pray for the soul of John Fitzgerald Kennedy. We were good Catholics, so we prayed. He was, after all, one of ours, the first Catholic President, and weren't we the smug little mackerel-snappers.

Thirty years have slipped by so fast since that afternoon. Conspiracy cranks, the same kind of people who used to play Beatle records backwards to hear "Paul is dead" messages, continue to write books and analyze blurry photographs, obsessively looking for some new clue. This was the most public murder in history and yet . . . we still don't know what really happened in Dealey Plaza.

Well, that's what keeps the Assassination Industry going, isn't it? The "official" version of what happened is clearly full of holes; but by now we've heard so many crackpot conspiracy theories that they've become meaningless, a self-perpetuating joke. I keep expecting an Assassination board game from Parker Brothers (who are, as everyone knows, a front for the CIA).

It's hard to convey to those too young to remember it, or who only know about it from Oliver Stone's rather hysterical movie, just how profoundly shocking Jack Kennedy's murder was. Try to imagine it: the most powerful, most popular man in the world—the President of the United States, for God's sake—shot down like a dog—in an American city—in broad daylight—in front of a crowd of people! It was impossible, unthinkable! It was reality on the skids!

Since then, of course, we've lived through one public assassination after another, and we've gotten used to them. In fact, we've come to expect them. Such is our world, thirty years later.

But the Kennedy assassination is still the most compelling. No amount of after-the-fact theorizing, no amount of investigative double-think, can alter the image frozen forever by Abraham Zapruder's camera—that single heartbreaking moment when Jack Kennedy's head blew apart, and all the dreams and hopes he inspired blew apart with it.

Of course, we didn't know then that he was a compulsive womanizer and a reckless risk-taker. Revisionist historians, infected by the tabloid mentality that now masquerades as journalism, have gleefully raked up all the dirty details and spit them in our faces. Well, all of that may be true, but it's also true that he was one of the few public figures of our time who actually inspired people. What a concept! Even here in little St. John's, Newfoundland—about as far away from Camelot as you could be—we, too, were inspired by Jack Kennedy.

And if the inspiration was murdered with him, maybe that's why we continue to cling to this irrational belief . . . that if we could just understand those six fatal seconds, if we could only penetrate the mystery inside the riddle inside the enigma . . . maybe then we could make some sense out of everything that's happened since.

Back in Grade Nine, at Brother Rice . . . well, we were all pretty quiet for the rest of the afternoon. I went home after school and, like the rest of the world, I spent the whole week-end glued to the TV, in a state of shock. There would be more horrors to come in the years ahead, but there was nothing quite like that week-end in hell, when reality itself seemed to go haywire.

Even my Cousin Ted was subdued, for a change. But he's had thirty years to mull it over and he has his own theory. "I know who shot JFK," says Ted. "It wasn't the Mafia or the CIA or the Cubans. It was . . . the Faeries. The Faeries killed Kennedy."

Hey, go prove him wrong.

For Week End A. M., I'm Absolutely Frank.

November 1993

Dirt

"Genial Johnny Murphy" was, of course, St. John's Mayor John Murphy. Patrick O'Flaherty is a former English professor-turned-media columnist. Patt Cowan was, at that time, the provincial Minister responsible for the environment. SNAGG was a citizen's group formed to protest the importation of American garbage (yes, Virginia, someone actually thought it'd be a good idea to import American garbage to Newfoundland!).

Remember when our license plates used to read: "Newfoundland—The Happy Province"? Well, I don't know how happy we actually were, but we must have been happier than we are now. However, I have a suggestion for a new license plate slogan. How's this? "Newfoundland—The Dirty Province."

Cripes, you can't step ten feet in any direction without tripping over someone's garbage, whether it's the abandoned car wrecks that still dot the roadsides from Cape Spear to Port aux Basques or the apparently endless supply of discarded bottles, chip bags and bar wrappers that blankets the landscape. There's so much litter lining the streets of St. John's, I figure it must serve as some kind of urban insulation. The one that kills me is when you come across, usually in the middle of a Mall parking lot, a pile of cigarette butts some slob has dumped out of his car ashtray. I mean, how friggin' lazy can you get? If you can't get it together to dump it in a trash bin, you could at least wait till you get home and dump it in your own garbage.

Why are we so dirty? And it's not just townies, either, although St. John's is one of the dirtiest cities in North America. No, we all just toss our crap away wherever we happen to be standing or walking or driving—kinda like the way a dog or a horse will just let go with a pile of steaming dung wherever they happen to be, utterly oblivious to any sense of decency, decorum or civic responsibility.

Is education or upbringing (or the lack of them) the problem here? Why don't the schools teach a compulsory course on tidiness? Are any kids ever told by their parents *not* to heave the chip bag out the car window as they speed along the Trans-Canada? How are these same kids supposed to learn anything when Dad is dumping his ashtray out in the street while he's stopped at a red light?

If Newfoundland is a pigsty, though, townies are the prime porkers. You go downtown on a Saturday or Sunday morning in St. John's and you practically have to wade through the broken beer bottles, the squashed remains of half-eaten French fries and occasional splatters of vomit. But don't think for a minute that the rest of Newfoundland is exempt: if you got dropped by helicopter smack in the middle of the Witless Bay Barrens, you'd probably land on some moron's empty six-pack or pizza box.

Maybe we're just naturally dirty. We've been accused and found guilty of everything else by the mainlanders, so we might as well confess to that too. We have nothing left to lose anyway, so okay, let's admit it: we *are* lazy and shiftless. To hell with the Quebecois, *we're* the real white niggers of Canada, so shag it—we're dirty too.

Say it loud and say it proud: we are dirty Newfoundlanders! We don't care about cleanliness or Godliness! We are not a bunch of uptight Protestant Nova Scotians! Jeez, you go to Nova Scotia and it's as clean as a whistle, you could practically eat off the streets. Who wants that? Not us! Damn it, it's our God-given birthright as Irish bums to throw our garbage anywhere we please. It's part of our charm! Properly marketed, it could become a major tourist attraction. How about submarine tours of St. John's Harbour, for instance? With Genial Johnny Murphy, in a lead-lined diving suit, as your guide? For those with an interest in Interactive Tourism, we could supply them (for a tidy profit, of course) with special "Newfoundland Garbage" (including used condoms and remaindered copies of *The Wit and Wisdom of Patrick O'Flaherty*) that they could fling into the streets themselves. Never mind SNAGG and the rest of those left-wing do-gooders! Let's turn Long Harbour into a giant blast-furnace and give those Yankee tourists a real show for their money. Florida can keep its Universal Studios theme park— what's a few mechanical dinosaurs and sharks compared to a mountain of flaming crud? The possibilities are endless—we could become the Disneyland of Dirt!

Patt Cowan be damned, we don't care about any bloody environmental clean-up! Let the garbage fall where it may! We are free Newfoundlanders! Free to be the slobs God and Nature intended us to be!

Hey, hand me that Styrofoam coffee cup and open the window—I've got a sudden urge to toss something somewhere.

For Week-End A. M., I'm Absolutely Filthy Frank.

March 1994

Calling Cousin Ted on the Unemployment Line

Stranger-Than-Fiction Department, Part Two: CBC producer Ingrid Fraser showed me the actual newspaper item about "Carscap Consulting" that inspired this piece. Golly, what next?

Re: the reference to Cashin Avenue—it used to have a tough reputation, but I'm assured that it's a relatively normal neighbourhood these days. No disrespect intended!

SOUND: FRANK HUMS "IT'S A LONG WAY TO TIPPERARY" AS HE DIALS A TELEPHONE. WE HEAR THE PHONE RINGING AT THE OTHER END, THEN BEING PICKED UP.

Hello, Ted? It's Frank. Yeah, absolutely. Are you awake? Good. Of course *I'm* awake, Ted, I wouldn't be . . . uh, never mind. Listen, I've got good news and I've got bad news. No, Ted, it's not a joke. No, first, the good news—I think I may have found the perfect solution to your . . . uh, problem. Yeah, I know that, Ted, but I also know you haven't had a real job in decades . . . yes, I'm counting the year you spent inserting bristles into toothbrushes. Yeah, I know that too, but . . . listen, working in a fish plant for an afternoon just wasn't enough to qualify you for The Package. It was a scam, Ted—you know it and I know it, and so does the government.

Anyway, Ted . . . Hazel showed me this thing in the paper, it sounds like it might be right up your alley. There's this company in Ottawa—Carscap Consulting—no, I don't know what it means. Well, they're hiring people to work over in Europe—yeah . . . well, wait now, let me finish—the jobs pay up to Sixty Grand a year . . . that's U. S. dollars, Ted . . . plus six weeks of holidays and free medical insurance. They're looking for suckers—er, people—to be secretaries, drivers, airport workers, or . . . well, just about anything, really—garbage men, dog catchers, collection agents, convenience store clerks. . .

This sounds like a golden opportunity, Ted. Yes, I'm serious . . . listen, I don't think you can afford to be too choosy . . . you wanna be forced to retrain as a computer zombie like all those fishermen? Here's a heaven-sent chance to collect a nice fat pay cheque, with top stamps at the end of it all. Sounds good, wha'?

The bad news? Oh. Well, the bad news is—the jobs are in Bosnia.

Now, wait a minute, Ted, don't say "No" until you hear the whole story. So you'd be dropped smack in the middle of a war zone—big deal! You should be used to that up on Cashin Avenue. Do you have to be so negative all the time?

Listen, these Carscap fellas insist that none of their workers have been injured or killed yet. Oh sure, some of them have had a few "close calls," but hey . . . what's life without a few risks? They're looking for people with a sense of adventure! People like you, Ted!

And don't forget those fringe benefits: the free medical insurance . . . well, in case you lose any essential body parts. . . the six weeks of holidays . . . in Rwanda, I hear . . . a great salary, and good U.I. at the end of it—if you live to collect it. And as if that's not enough, you get to live in a bombed-out hotel or your very own 6 x 18 foot "container"—with doors and windows! Well, cripes, Ted, considering that rat-infested hell-hole you live in now, it could only be an improvement. You could finally tell Newfoundland Housing where to shove it.

Picture it, Ted—a full year of living in a box in Bosnia! No, no, they'll provide you with a free helmet and a flak jacket. Just think of the stories you can tell if you come back! The bombs, the bullets, the camaraderie, the genocide—Gee, you could finally write that novel you've always been planning.

What's that? No, Ted . . . I know what it sounds like, but I don't think this is a Reform Party scheme to eliminate the unemployed by shipping them off to certain death. On the other hand, y'know, it could get rid of a lot of ungrateful whiners who probably don't deserve to be Canadians. What? Oh, don't worry, you won't be alone—it says in the paper that at least thirty thrill-seeking Newfoundlanders have signed up already.

So whaddya say, Ted? Well, it's too late now, I already put your name in. What? I know you're my cousin, Ted, but that's a just a genetic accident. I'll be over in twenty minutes to help you pack. And dress light—they say Sarajevo is just like the Riviera in the summer.

'Bye 'bye. Oh, and listen, Ted—stay in touch.

SOUND: FRANK HANGS UP THE PHONE AND SINGS CONTENTEDLY TO HIMSELF.

"It's a long way to Sarajevo, it's a long way to go . . ."

April 1994

Absolutely Frank Gets Goosebumps and Goes Home

"Goosebumps" is the name of a record-spin show on CBC Radio in St. John's, hosted by a variety of people. When producer Jamie Fitzpatrick asked me to do one, I couldn't resist the temptation to drag Frank into it—it seemed like a good opportunity to gripe about several things at once. Incidentally, this was the first mention by name of Frank's wife Hazel.

As for the songs indicated in the script, you'll just have to hum them to yourself.

Good afternoon. I'm Absolutely Frank—welcome to my world.

SOUND: WINDOW SMASHING, FOLLOWED BY A LOUD YELP OF PAIN.

Frankly, I don't listen to the radio all that much—too damn noisy for me. I don't like the music, and those disc jockey voices go through my brain like an ice-pick. I prefer to watch TV with the sound turned down—you can't really do that with radio, though . . .

Now don't get me wrong—I have nothing against radio—in fact, some of my best friends are radios. But let's face it —there are radios and there are radios, and, despite what the Constitution says, all radios are not created equal. Radios used to be all right—they knew their place and they kept to it. Now all you hear is a lot of whining about "Radio Rights" and "Radio Empowerment"—Jeez, everywhere you turn these days, there's a damn radio in your face, demanding the right to this or that—it's enough to make a white male Anglo-Saxon heterosexual puke.

Before I beat this clumsy metaphor to death, let me remind you of one simple fact—if you don't like what you hear on the radio, you can always turn it off. If only everything in life were that simple! Bigots like me would be in Paradise.

MUSIC: "FM" (Steely Dan)

Just kidding, folks. I'm no bigot. *Au contraire*—I'm full of love for everyone, regardless of race, creed, religion, sexual orientation, age, hair style, fashion sense, or mental capacity.

My Cousin Ted, on the other hand, is a kind of egalitarian bigot—he dislikes everyone equally. As far as Ted is concerned, the entire population could be abducted by aliens tomorrow and he wouldn't care. It'd just mean more beer for him.

Actually, Ted doesn't believe in aliens, and he's not convinced there's life on this planet, either. Ted subscribes to the Cosmic Ice Theory—the idea that the earth and the sun are inside a huge hollow ball surrounded by a limitless expanse of Cosmic Ice.

Hey, stop laughing—Ted didn't make this up. He shares this theory with several other notable cosmologists, including those sons of fun, Hermann Goering and Heinrich Himmler. Oh, those wacky Nazis! And these clowns were gonna rule the world! *Ach du lieber!*

Speaking of clowns . . . I have had it up to here with neo-Nazi pinheads like the Ernst Zundls of the world, the kind of clucks who go around insisting that the Holocaust never happened. "Oh sure," they say, "lots of Jews died, but hey—there was a war on, lots of people died."

Well then, Ernst, tell me this—where did all those Jews go? You can't just misplace six million people like they were lost cuff-links or something. The Germans used to pretend that they didn't know what was going on . . . but surely they must have wondered occasionally. I mean, if your town had a Jewish population, ordinary respectable citizens, businessmen, doctors, lawyers, and suddenly one day they were *all gone*—wouldn't you notice? Wouldn't you wonder what became of all those Jews who used to live down the street? Funny, you don't see them around anymore. Oh well, I guess they all moved away. Pass the pumpernickel, Ernst.

MUSIC: "DER FUHRER'S FACE" (Spike Jones)

Grunt and flex and squat and flex and grunt and . . .

Everyone's exercising and dieting and working out like the Hitler Youth these days. The theory behind all this huffing and puffing and sweating is, I suppose, that we could all end up looking like Cindy Crawford or Michael Jordan if only we squatted and grunted and stretched and abdominized enough.

Aside from the obvious commercial benefits to those who sell this Aryan Fitness philosophy, I've got to wonder who it's all for. Gullible yuppies with money, I guess—people who can be intimidated into believing that unless they are physically perfect, their lives simply aren't worth living.

When I was a kid, it was Charles Atlas who promised to change us all from 98 lb. weaklings into virile he-men. Just follow the Dynamic Tension Plan, and next time some smirking, bullet-headed bully kicks sand in your face, you can spring up from your beach-blanket and pound the bejesus out of him. And hey, fellas, your gal will love you for it!

Let's get a grip, shall we? Why should we believe that perfect health will make us better people? What do you do when you've attained the peak of physical health and realize that you're still a boring, obnoxious clod?

So I've got a few extra pounds on me—so what? Every one of them is honestly come by, and I wear my flab with a certain stubborn pride. I tried those stupid 5 BX exercises once and all I got for it was a dislocated shoulder.

MUSIC: "FAT" (Weird Al Yankovich)

SOUND: A PACK OF BARKING DOGS.

Council will come to order!

SOUND: BARKING DOGS SUBSIDE.

Just before last Christmas, the endomorphs who run the

City Pound got their knickers in a knot because Debbie Powers of the SPCA called them a bunch of "illiterates." The dog catchers' union reared up on its hind legs and snarled in outrage. "Who do she t'ink she is, callin' us illiterates, callin' us the bottom of the municipal barrel? Grrr! Arf! Arf! Are we not men? If ye pricks us, do we not bleed?"

Ah, Debbie obviously don't know what she's talkin' about. Sure, everyone knows the City Pound is run by retired rocket scientists, former Cabinet Ministers and members of MENSA. God, yes. Drivin' that truck around town, chasin' after those friggin' dogs—by Jesus, it looks easy, but, as Winnie the Pooh's friend Piglet says, it's not everyone who could do it.

If the dog catchers wanted to perform a *real* public service, they ought to stake out the City Council meetings. You can tune in to Channel 9 any old time and see our very own elected gang of human crackies yapping and snarling at each other around the Council table. I haven't actually seen any of 'em lifting their legs to take a leak or sniffing each other's behinds—but maybe they wait till the cameras are off before they do that.

Well, anyway, God bless the guys at the Pound, they're doin' a grand job. All those years of studying and training have paid off. And they stand as a fine example to all those students struggling to get through high school and university—there's a career waiting for you, kids! Get that degree and join the ranks! And bring a heavy pair of gloves.

MUSIC: "DOG EAT DOG" (Steely Dan)

Do dogs go to heaven? I sure hope so. I can think of at least half a dozen dogs I'd like to see again. In fact, there are probably more dogs I'd like to see again than there are people.

That raises an interesting question, though—did Jesus like dogs? The Gospels are silent on the subject, but I'd like to think He did. I think about Jesus a lot, actually. I think about things like: did He have cavities or, being the Son of God, did he have perfect teeth? Again, the Gospels don't say.

Actually, the Gospels don't say much, when you think

about it. They don't even tell us what Jesus looked like. In fact, we only have the Gospels' word for it that He existed at all.

I know I, for one, was very disappointed when it turned out that the Shroud of Turin only dates back to the 13th or 14th century. Damn! I guess I was secretly hoping that it would prove authentic—it would have been some kind of proof, if not that it's the actual burial cloth of Jesus, then at least that it could be.

So where does that leave us? As with all religions, we either believe or we don't believe. I think it's called "faith." I'm not sure I have much faith in "faith," myself. It's not so much that I don't believe as that I don't believe in believing, if you see what I mean. If you lock yourself into any system of belief, whether it's Christianity, Yogic Flying or a Fruit-and-Fibre Diet, you're deliberately ignoring all other possibilities, and I don't think God would want me to do that.

I still have a soft spot for Jesus, though. He was a hell of a guy, no doubt about it. Even Cousin Ted likes Him, and Ted is a fanatical agnostic, the kind of lapsed Catholic who wants to lapse other Catholics. As Ted likes to say, "Keep on comin' Jesus, you're the best-dressed."

MUSIC: "(WE'VE BEEN TOLD) JESUS COMIN' SOON"
(Eric Clapton)

I don't know how Jesus felt about personal relationships—He didn't say, and, aside from some nasty gossip about Mary Magdelene, the Gospels don't give any evidence that He ever had any.

I don't have any personal relationships, myself, unless you count Hazel and the kids and Cousin Ted. They're quite enough to deal with, thank you very much.

I know this much, though, from bitter experience—it's a big mistake to try to live your life according to the lyrics of your favourite love songs. I love you a bushel and a peck, a bushel and a peck and a hug around the neck. Love is blue. Love me do. Love is a many-splendoured thing. Let's do it, let's fall in love.

Love hurts. All you need is love. Why do fools fall in love?

I think it was Kurt Vonnegut who said that saying "I love you" is like holding a loaded gun to someone's head—they have no choice, if they want to live, but to say "I love you, too." Love is simply too dangerous to be left to amateurs, so don't try it at home.

People say to me, "Frank, you're so cynical. Haven't you ever been in love?" Well, sure, of course I have. Before I met Hazel I was in love all the time. I was in love so much I developed a rash.

Believe it or not, it was Cousin Ted who introduced me to Hazel. She was a counselor at his halfway house, and Ted used to phone me up all the time to tell me he'd found the perfect woman for me. I didn't believe him, of course—Ted is usually attracted to women who are too much like Ted for my taste.

But when I finally met Hazel at Ted's parole hearing, I knew right away we were meant for each other. Sounds corny, but it's true. She resisted at first—she was wary of anyone related to Ted. I could understand that—I felt the same way.

But eventually I wore her down, we got married, and my rash cleared up. Hazel is more of a realist than I am. She said, "Frank, love is all very nice, but what's more important is who you can stand to talk to every day of your life, who can put up with you when no one else will."

Maybe that's why Ted never got married.

MUSIC: "YOU DON'T SAY" (Richard Thompson).
ESTABLISH AND CONTINUE UNDER.

(Over the music) Well, folks, I have to run—Hazel's making cabbage rolls tonight and I don't want to miss that. For *Goosebumps*, I'm Absolutely Fra—

SOUND: LOUD SQUEAL OF FEEDBACK.

What the . . .? Ted? What are you doing here? You know the judge said you're not supposed to come within five hundred yards of me! Who let him in here? Someone call the cops! Ted! Leave those knobs alone! Ted!!!

SOUND: LOUD CRASHING NOISE, CRIES OF PAIN, GENERAL MAYHEM, ETC. AS TAPE SPOOL SPEEDS UP AND FINALLY BREAKS.

May 1994

Jocks, Big Bucks & the Ted Factor

MUSIC: THE HOCKEY SONG (Stompin' Tom Connors)
AAAAH, SHADDAPP!!! *(à la Daffy Duck)*
MUSIC: ENDS ABRUPTLY.

Good morning, sports fans. The Stanley Cup has been won and the hockey season is finally over—in June, no less! I will now risk being publicly disemboweled at centre-ice by a mob of moronic sports fans like the one that demolished downtown Vancouver on Tuesday night simply because, *(Heavily sarcastic sookiness)* boo hoo, their team lost. Sniff, sniff.

Well, here goes—this is one little black duck who doesn't share the hysterical obsession with sports that has our nation and our TV networks in a stranglehold. There, I've said it, and I feel better for it. From where I sit on my comfy living room couch, I feel like I'm being tortured to death by an endlessly revolving cycle of televised sports. It's like being trapped inside one of those little exercise wheels with an insane hamster.

When I was a kid, I was vaguely interested in hockey and basketball, thanks mostly to Foster Hewitt and the Harlem Globetrotters. And then, guess what, folks? *I grew up!* I got more interested in things like books, movies, music and . . . girls. To hell with *Hockey Night in Canada!* There were better things to do on a Saturday night.

Some people, however, never grow up. Which brings me, inevitably, to my Cousin Ted. Cousin Ted, surprisingly enough, is something of a sports *aficionado.* I say "surprisingly" because, to my knowledge, the closest Ted has ever come to any kind of athletic event is twisting the caps off bottles of Jockey Club. If there was an Olympic Bottle Cap Twist-Off, Ted could probably win all three medals with every one of his limbs tied behind his back. He could still use his teeth, after all.

Now, when faced with the spectacle of Ted in his grubby singlet slumped in front of the TV watching the play-offs or the kick-offs or the throw-offs, amid a stinking pile of empty beer bottles and overflowing ashtrays, belching, grunting and rooting for "his" team, I'm reminded of many things—Romans and gladiators, orangutans in heat—but the one thing I'm not reminded of is anything even remotely athletic. Ted, like so many rabid sports fans, hasn't got an athletic bone in his beer-bellied body.

That physical disparity between sports fans and actual athletes is ludicrous enough, but what really burns my bird is the obscene amounts of money these big gum-chewing, tobacco-spitting, inarticulate pituitary freaks make. Cripes, they're paid millions of dollars to do the only thing they're physically suited for besides construction work. If there were any justice in the world, someone like Ted would be paid millions simply to sit around and scratch.

I'll tell you what I do like to watch, though—snooker tournaments. I don't know if you can call snooker a "sport," exactly, but there's great skill involved, and the champs always dress so nice. I also like to watch those horse-jumping events—the horses are beautiful to look at, and the riders also dress real nice. I don't know how much money those people make, but their outfits must cost a pretty penny, and, buddy, they're worth every cent.

As for the rest of it—hockey, baseball, football, basketball, soccer, golf, you name it—I must stifle a yawn and switch to the City Council meetings on Channel 9. Those players are overpaid, dress badly, look more like Cousin Ted than Michael Jordan and have no apparent talent for anything other than name-calling . . . but they're pretty darn entertaining, all the same.

For Week-End A. M., I'm Absolutely Frank.

June 1994

PART TWO

Here, There and Everywhere

Frank expands his grumpy horizons and rants about *The Evening Telegram,* the federal deficit, Christmas, the banks and mainlanders; meanwhile his personal life begins to intrude, and Cousin Ted enters public life.

Fax from François

This piece was inspired by the radical actions of the citizens of François, a small community on Newfoundland's isolated South Coast, who detained the coastal boat Marine Runner *for several days in protest against its owners' plans to reduce the ferry service, their only connection to the outside world.* Here and Now *is the local CBC TV evening news show.*

In retrospect, this piece marks an interesting turning point: from here on, the Franks gradually began to turn away from straightforward commentary and become more personal.

So Hazel's got these friends from the States, see, Harvey and Rochelle, and they're up here for a visit, first time they've ever set foot out of California. So they're gawking around town, and I'm thinking "If they say 'New*found*land' one more time, I'm gonna strangle them and hide their bodies in Pippy Park." Now, Hazel and I have been married for donkey's years, so she knows exactly when I'm about to spontaneously combust. She comes up with a great idea—she'll take these Yuppie Yanks on a coastal boat trip, show them some of the "real" Newfoundland! Yowza! That oughta be fun!

Well, the good news is—they want to go. The bad news is—they want to take my Cousin Ted with them. Yipes! Despite all our efforts to avoid Ted, he drops over to the house one night, trying to get me to co-sign for a bank loan (some hopes, Ted!), and meets Harvey and Rochelle. Imagine our dismay when Harvey unexpectedly takes a shine to Ted. He says Ted reminds him of his campus radical/Haight-Ashbury days and it's great to see someone "keeping the flame alive." I swear, that's what he said. Of course, Harvey is now an overweight record company lawyer being investigated by the IRS, but he likes to pretend he's still Harvey the Hippie from 'Frisco. Hazel tries to warn Harvey about Ted, to no avail. Harvey ties his remaining hair in an obscene little ponytail, steps into his Birkenstocks and proclaims Ted his "main man."

Anyway, off they go on a Friday, on the *Marine Runner* to the sunny South Coast, Newfoundland's very own Riviera. I breathe a sigh of relief—until I see *Here and Now* on Monday. A couple of days later, I get this frantic Fax from Hazel in François:

> "Dear Frank, (it begins) you are really in for it this time, mister. If I ever get out of here, I'm going to eviscerate you, your insane cousin and your whole misbegotten family. It's not bad enough that I'm forced to be stuck here with Ted—oh no, I have to listen to Harvey and Ted reminisce about the Sixties until I feel like my head's going to fall off. To hear them tell it, they single-handedly organized Woodstock and stopped the Vietnam War. Our first night at sea, Ted and Harvey had a snootful of Screech and tried to suck all the passengers into having a Love-In—Harvey was singing 'White Rabbit' while Ted played some kid's Casio portable keyboard.
>
> "Next morning, Ted is up trying to convince the ship's Captain to let him steer the boat. He tells the Captain he's on a secret mission for Marine Atlantic and it's his job to find out—these are his exact words—'how well this old bucket handles a bit of stress.' I pretended I didn't know him, but the Captain told me if Ted caused any more trouble, he'd have him keelhauled. They don't still do that, do they, Frank?
>
> "I could have ignored all that as long as we were still moving, but when these bloody baymen decided to hold us hostage, Ted suddenly emerged as a social agitator—he jumps ship and starts helping 'his brothers in the struggle'—that's what he called them, Frank, and you know as well as I do Ted's only struggle in life has been to stay out of jail long enough to collect two welfare cheques in a row.

"So there's Ted on the wharf, waving one clenched fist in the air, and Harvey is singing 'Solidarity Forever'—I think he's going through a particularly irritating Mid-Life Crisis—and the locals are starting to get scared of them. Meantime the crew and the other passengers are going stir-crazy, fist-fights are breaking out, and they're giving me and Rochelle the most unfriendly looks. It's a good thing I didn't tell them I was married to you, Frank, that might have sent them right over the edge.

"I have to stop now. Ted just snuck up on me to say we're going to make a break for it tonight, even if he has to take the wheel himself. Frank? I'm worried."

And that's where the Fax ends. Gee, I hope Hazel's okay. I know they got away that night, but I haven't heard from her. I'm not sure if that's good or bad. The only thing I can't figure out is—who the hell owns a Fax machine in François?

For Week-End A. M., I'm Absolutely Frank. Or, as they say in François, I'm Absolutely François.

July 1994

Diamonds are Forever, but so is Cousin Ted

This and several other commentaries reveal that provincial Cabinet Minister Chuck Furey is a favourite target of Frank's ridicule. I'm not sure why.

Before they found out the hard way just what Cousin Ted is really like, my wife Hazel's nitwit friends, Harvey and Rochelle from California, called him "a diamond in the rough." Yeah, right. In school, a succession of hair-pulling guidance counselors put it this way: "Ted is not living up to his potential." Ted's father, Ted Senior, put it more bluntly. "Ted," he'd say, "you've got a long way to go in life . . . now get the hell out of my house." Ted interpreted this as an omen, the first step on the path towards his inscrutable Destiny.

The other day, Ted calls me up and asks me to co-sign for a bank loan. After I calmed down enough to speak, I said, "Ted, are you mad? Have you lost whatever's left of your mind? You have no income, no credit rating, and there's no way you're using me as a credit reference. Besides, Hazel would skin me alive. What the hell do you want a bank loan for, anyway?"

Ted tries a few evasionary tactics, but I finally pin him down. He says he needs a "grubstake" so he can go to Labrador and get in on the ground floor of what he referred to as "this diamond mining scam." I said, "Ted, are you mad? Diamonds? In Labrador? Have you been taking Chuck Furey seriously again? Besides, not only do you not know a thing about diamond mining, I doubt if anyone is gonna let you go wandering around Labrador with a pick and shovel, digging for diamonds or anything else. You'd be better off digging up peat moss. At least you know what it looks like."

Ted is highly insulted and says he can recognize a diamond when he sees it. I said, "Ted, are you mad? Do you think they're gonna be lying around on the ground like rabbit pellets? We're talking major excavation here, huge machines, hundreds of sweating miners. What the hell is it with you? What are you really after?"

And here's where he stumps me, folks. He says he wants to take a fistful of diamonds to Rome and offer them to the Pope in return for a plenary indulgence. Now, for the benefit of Our Separated Brethren of the Protestant Persuasion, I should explain that a plenary indulgence means nothing less than the remission of all temporal punishment for your sins—in other words, time off for good behaviour, no hard labour in Purgatory before you can skeet your way into heaven. For a Serial Sinner like Ted, this is the spiritual equivalent of winning the 649.

After a *very* long pause, I said, "Ted, are you mad? Who do you think you are, Frank Sinatra? If bribing the Pope didn't work for Ol' Blue Eyes, what makes you think it'll work for you? And how would you get to Rome in the first place?"

Well, Ted has come up with a hell of a scheme—he 's gonna offer himself as a tour guide to this local family that's got an audience with the Pope! He's gonna go to the Vatican with them, pull the Pope aside at an opportune moment, shove the diamonds at him and make him an offer he can't refuse.

I said, "Ted, for the last time, are you mad? You can't guide anyone around Rome! You can't even find your way to the Village Mall without getting lost! And even if you did get to Rome, what are you gonna do when the Pope tells you to fly to hell?"

Well, Ted has a back-up plan. He calls it, with Ted-like simplicity, "Plan B." He says if the Pope won't give him the indulgence, he'll settle for a piece of the Holy Shroud or one of those nifty Swiss Guard outfits.

It was around that point that I hung up and started chewing

on my own tongue. Hazel came running into the room and asked me with admirable calm why I was pulling the phone wires out of the wall with my teeth. I tried to explain my conversation with Ted, but all I could manage to get out between sobs were the words, "Diamonds! Ted! Labrador! The Pope!" before I collapsed on the couch.

Hazel made me take a double dose of Prozac and pretty soon I didn't care about Ted or Labrador or diamonds, or . . . much of anything, really. I haven't heard from Ted since, but if the Pope ever places Newfoundland under a Papal Interdict—that means TOTAL EXCOMMUNICATION, with everyone in the province cast into the outer darkness, wailing and gnashing our teeth—well, I'll know who to blame.

For Week-End A. M., I'm Absolutely Stupefied Frank.

July 1994

Up Close and (Ugh!) Personal

The Ayres are one of those "old" St. John's families, bastions of the merchant class for several generations. Students of Newfoundland history will understand the resentment they and their kind provoke among us common folk.

SOUND: FRANK LEAFS THROUGH A NEWSPAPER, HUMMING "STRANGERS IN THE NIGHT" TO HIMSELF. HE STOPS AT THE PERSONAL COLUMNS.

Hmm. What have we here? *(He reads)* "Brutally handsome male, mid-20s to late-40s, with a hell of a sense of humour and all his own teeth, seeks feisty females, the younger the better, for erotic thrill-ride in the great outdoors. Come and get me, gals!"

So this is what "The People's Paper" has come to!

SOUND: HE TOSSES THE PAPER ASIDE IN DISGUST.

I read *The Evening Telegram* for one reason, and one reason only—it's the only game in town.

When Miller Ayre took over as Publisher and General Manager, I didn't exactly have high hopes—he *is* an Ayre, after all—but I thought, well, let's give him the benefit of the doubt. Maybe ol' Miller-time will take this soggy journalistic ball and run with it, kick some life into this stodgy old right-wing tool of the upper-class-townie status quo.

Alas, no. Miller's major innovation has turned out to be a feature called "The Meeting Place," a kind of Fourth Estate pimping service for lonely hearts who can't find a partner the same way the rest of us do. Why can't they use the time-honoured method of making a fool of yourself at parties, pretending to be smarter and funnier than you actually are, saying the wrong thing at the wrong time, or worse, saying the wrong thing at the right time and blowing whatever slim chance you had to begin with?

Now, God knows it's never easy to find a suitable companion of any gender with whom you can share some quality time and satisfy your sexual quirks. But, human nature being what it is, people do manage to get together without resorting to things like "The Meeting Place" and other artificial aids (although some people, I'm told, like to use a large rubber chicken).

Reading through these "personals," I find an alarming number of men and women who romantically describe themselves as liking "quiet, intimate evenings," "fun times" and, most commonly, "long walks." "Long walks?" This conjures up an image of hundreds, perhaps thousands, of lovesick Newfoundlanders constantly wandering around the landscape like herds of lonely, horny caribou.

As it happens, I'm a married caribou and my wandering days are over. I suppose if I hadn't met my wife, Hazel, in a perfectly normal way—well, actually, it was at my Cousin Ted's parole hearing, but that's another story—I might be tempted to run one of those ads myself. The trouble is, I'd have to be Absolutely Honest, and my ad would read: "Cranky middle-aged fuss-budget, going bald and running to fat, seeks woman with a high tolerance for loony relatives. Must be willing to answer the door and the phone and tell everyone I'm not home."

I asked Hazel if, knowing what she knows now, she'd respond to an ad like that, but she just gave me an enigmatic smile and went back to playing Mortal Kombat.

I went back to browsing through "The Meeting Place" until I came across this ad: "Chronically unemployed male, mid-40s, with a taste for beer, recreational drugs and shooting pool, seeks woman, or reasonable facsimile, with full-time job, as soulmate. Nude photo or videotape a must."

My suspicions were aroused. Hold on, I thought, I know that style—it's Cousin Ted! Ted has never been married, but he has had questionable relationships with a number of deluded women over the years. Those relationships always failed as soon as the women involved came to their senses or got professional help.

I called Ted right away and told him, "Ted, don't be so foolish—you don't need a woman, you need a job. I hear there's an opening at the Constabulary—Sam the Police Dog has passed on to that Great Cop Kennel in the Sky, and I think you oughta apply for his job. Jeez, Ted, you've got all the necessary qualifications—you can sniff out drugs better than any mutt, you're more comfortable on all fours and you're always scratching yourself. Besides, I think you'd actually make a better dog than you do a human being. Plus, you'd have no trouble finding female companionship. You could always proposition the RCMP's dog: 'Horny hound seeks bitch in heat. Object: canine cavorting.'"

For Week-End A. M., I'm Absolutely Frank.

September 1994

Cousin Ted Joins a Cult and Causes Trouble

Frank Moores and Brian Peckford were, of course, P.C. Premiers of Newfoundland during the 70s.

Your average Newfoundlander, sound of mind and body, is temperamentally unsuited to taking orders, especially from another Newfoundlander. More often than not, when ordered to do something, a Newfoundlander may say, "Like ducks!" or, even more commonly, "No, b'y, I can't." This probably explains why cults have never made much headway here.

Despite the media's breathless fascination with them, cults are nothing new. The Nazis were a cult, after all, as were the Communists. What is Christianity but a cult that grew and grew until it got completely out of hand? Same goes for Islam, the Loyal Order of the Elk, the Shriners, the Mormons, the Knights of Columbus, the NDP . . . well, you get the idea.

My Cousin Ted, always in the forefront of foolishness, tried to join a few cults, looking for free beer and chicks, but not even the Moonies would have him. About twenty years ago, though, Ted did temporarily infiltrate a local chapter of the Rastafarians. For those unfamiliar with the Rasta philosophy, let me briefly explain:

The Rastas started in Jamaica as a group of socio-religious zealots who believed that the late Emperor of Ethiopia, Hailie Selasse, was the embodiment of the living God. Uh huh. Aside from the music of Bob Marley, this particular cult was noted for its severe vegetarianism and the sacramental use of enormous quantities of *ganja*, or marijuana. Hey, a sacrament is a sacrament, okay?

In the mid-70s, a charter branch of the Rastas emerged in St. John's, of all places. A small band of white, Catholic townies grew their limp Caucasian hair into lumpy dreadlocks and smoked themselves into a sacramental stupor while grooving to round-the-clock reggae. They summarily dismissed all non-Rastas as "pus-bags" and devoted endless hours to intense discussions of their bowel movements.

Insular and self-obsessed? You bet, but they were generally harmless. Ted, that relentless dope-hound, sniffed them out and, sure enough, soon started growing dreadlocks and calling me and my wife Hazel "a couple of pus-bags." Hazel is not one to take kindly to that sort of thing, nor would she tolerate Ted's flagrant flatulence, a noxious by-product of the Rasta diet. The other Rastas also quickly tired of Ted's foul emanations, as well as his monomaniacal insistence that "ska" and "reggae" weren't the same thing at all, mon. Ted was excommunicated, or given the boot.

So he started his own cult. He attracted a handful of followers, who went around talking like Ted, walking like Ted, dressing like Ted . . . brrr! It was scary. They called themselves "The Royal Knights of the Living Ted." They consumed large quantities of sacramental Jockey Club. They began making a nuisance of themselves at Torbay Airport, shaking tambourines and hustling for spare change. Tourism began to suffer. Questions were asked in the House of Assembly. Frank Moores and Brian Peckford both disavowed any knowledge of Ted or his minions, but it is suspected that the resulting uproar was at least partly responsible for the fall of the Moores government and Peckford's subsequent history of nervous breakdowns.

In the end, Ted's own followers threw him out of the cult, claiming that he was simply too disgusting to take seriously, and besides, he seemed to be spending a suspicious amount of time "anointing" his female devotees and collecting arbitrary membership fees. They disbanded, and many of them joined the Cult of the Young Liberals. Ted successfully de-programmed himself and went on vacation to Jamaica—until the Rastas there demanded he be deported.

The moral of the story? Ted failed as a cult member because he couldn't stand anyone telling him what to do. He failed as a cult leader because, except when he was loaded drunk or stoned as a rat and speaking in tongues, or "Ted-speak," he couldn't think of a damn thing to tell his followers. People get tired of that sort of thing after a while.

I've often thought of starting a cult of my own, but, as Groucho Marx put it, I wouldn't want to belong to any group that would have someone like me as a member.

For Week-End A M., I'm Absolutely Anti-social Frank.

October 1994

How I Learned To Stop Worrying and Love the Deficit

Paul Martin is the Federal Finance Minister. Vince Withers was the CEO of the Newfoundland Telephone Company.

My wife Hazel and I were recently picking through the monthly bills, trying to figure out which creditors we could pay and how much we could pay 'em—y'know, just to keep 'em off our backs for another month, or another week.

We usually perform this unholy ritual in my "office," which is actually a small room in the basement full of suitcases and empty boxes. By calling it an "office in the home," however, I can deduct certain expenses at tax time, since, according to Revenue Canada, I'm "self-employed." That means I don't have a regular job or a regular salary. Get this—I'm trying to make a living as a writer—in Newfoundland! I must be insane! Well, no—I'm "self-employed," which amounts to the same thing.

Hazel comes down with the mail—a cut-off notice from those bloodsuckers at the Light & Power Company—and says, "Good news, Frank! Paul Martin is on TV saying he's gonna get the federal deficit under control no matter how much it hurts! Yippee!" Well, that *is* good news. God knows I've spent many a sleepless night gnashing my teeth over the federal deficit. Why, it's all I can do to get out of bed in the mornings, I get so wrought up about it.

With a bitter chuckle, Hazel says, "Personally, I think he's on the right track. It's high time you, me and everyone else in this pampered country bite the bullet and choke on it. I mean, honestly, Frank, do we really need the Porsche and the Jacuzzi and the vacations in Aruba? Do the kids really need to go to Harlow instead of MUN?"

I tear up the Light & Power bill and ask, "Just how does Mr Martin intend to perform this miracle, Hazel, my pet?" "I'm not sure," says Hazel with a slap-happy grin, "but I think I heard him say something about 'loaves and fishes.' And here's the best part, Frank—he says we're all gonna have to tighten our belts!"

Well, we laugh and laugh. "Again?" I say. I've tightened my belt so much in the last few years that I've nearly bisected myself. Then I had to sell all my belts just so I could afford to keep my pants.

"But Hazel," I say, "is Mr Martin gonna tighten his belt, too?" "He won't have to, Frank," she chortles, "he wears suspenders." After a brief fit of hysterical giggling, I wipe away my tears and say, "You know something, Hazel? I'd bet you a buck, if I had one, that all the politicians, corporate CEOs and unemployed millionaires who make buckets of money and milk the system for all the perks they can get—I bet they'll all volunteer to take huge pay cuts! Just watch! They'll want to do their part to help get our fiscal house in order! After all, what's good for the country is good for business, isn't it?"

"I think you've got that backwards, Frank," says Hazel, as she rips up a Telephone Company bill. She puts the pieces in an envelope and addresses it to Vince Withers, whom we affectionately think of as "Prune Face."

"Hazel, my dove," I say as I set fire to a Revenue Canada bill, "how naive are you, at all? Surely our elected politicians and business leaders won't simply stand by and let ordinary people, people like us, sell our homes or eat cat food just so their balance sheets can look nice and tidy? Good God, woman, what kind of a country do you think we're living in?"

"That's a damn good question, Frank," says Hazel. Suddenly, the phone rings. It's my Cousin Ted, asking if he can borrow $100 so he can go video gambling. Oh, and could I send it over to him in a Gulliver's cab? He'd come and get it himself, only he's watching Paul Martin on TV explaining how we'll all be better off in the long run. Ted is laughing so hard I can barely make out a word he's saying as I hang up on him.

Hazel and I share a bowl of Purina Dog Chow for supper. Hazel spits out a tooth and says, "I know it tastes like crap, Frank, but it's better than the raw turkey gizzards we had last night. Let's face it—if we want to be fiscally responsible Canadians, I guess we'll just have to get used to making sacrifices. It's the future, Frank. Do we have any ketchup?"

I make a mental note to call the dentist and everyone else we owe money to and have them send the bills to Paul Martin.

For Week-End A.M., I'm Absolutely Flat-broke Frank.

(Sorry, Hazel—no ketchup.)

SOUND: FRANK NOISILY MUNCHES DRY DOG CHOW.

October 1994

I Left My Heart in the Balcony of the Capitol Theatre

This show is being broadcast from CBC Radio in beautiful downtown St. John's. Right behind the Radio building, facing Henry Street, is the old Capitol Theatre, a relic of the days when St. John's still had downtown movie houses—like the Nickel, the Star, the Majestic, the York and, of course, the fabulous Paramount Theatre on Harvey Road, the closest thing to a genuine St. John's "movie palace" that I can recall. I saw my first movie at the Paramount when I was five years old—I don't remember the movie now, but I do remember the theme song: "Hajii Baba, Hajii Baba, he was always in love." (My guess would be that the story involved someone named Hajii Baba.)

Alas, the Paramount closed twenty years ago, after the roof cracked during a showing of *Mary, Queen of Scots* (whoa! talk about a bad review!). That left the Capitol as our only downtown cinema, until, sadly, it, too, bit the bullet some years later. You know what? I still miss it. When we were kids, me and my Cousin Ted used to spend a lot of time up in the balcony at the Capitol—ah, what a magical phrase: "up in the balcony"! I'd be watching the movie, Ted would be balancing on the balcony railing or throwing popcorn boxes at the screen.

Eventually, CBC took over the building and installed a modern recording studio. One day shortly after that, I was blindly roaming the upstairs hallways at CBC, trying to find my way to the new studio. I wandered down a dark corridor, opened an unmarked door and found myself . . . in the lobby of the Capitol Theatre! Holy smokes! And nothing had changed! The ticket booth was still there, the same fausty red carpet was still on the floor, the intoxicating tang of rancid popcorn butter still hung in the air! It was like being inside a time capsule! And when I groped my way upstairs, I found the balcony completely intact, seats and all. My God, the memories came flooding back—this was where I traded comics at Saturday matinees! This was where I saw *A Hard Day's Night* for the first time! This was where, as a lovesick fifteen-year-old, I held sweaty hands with Sharon McKinley as we watched *Mary Poppins* together! This was where I tried, unsuccessfully, to cop a feel from Cindy Miller during an all-night Horrorama! Man, those were great days!

Going to the movies just isn't the same thrilling and glamorous experience it once was. For one thing, you used to be able to walk a few blocks to get to a movie. These days, if you don't have a car, you might as well try to organize a trip to Borneo as arrange to get out to the Malls. For another, most of your modern movie theatres, multiple mini-cineplexes stuck inside shopping malls, are bland little shoe boxes, with no character, no ambiance and no balconies—nothing to make "going to the movies" an opportunity to kindle any special memories . . .

Special memories . . . like Cousin Ted's practical jokes. (Well, he'd call them practical jokes when the cops arrived.) Ted's favourite gag was to get up in the balcony at the Capitol and pour a can of Campbell's vegetable soup onto people's heads, while he made puking noises. A laff riot, right? Well, Ted thought so, until he was barred from the Capitol for life.

Ted has since been barred-for-life from the Avalon Mall and the Topsail Cinemas as well. In a burst of nostalgic recidivism, he went to the Avalon Mall Cinema 1 and tried the vegetable soup trick anyway, balcony or no balcony. As he was hauled away by a brace of Mall security guards, Ted yelled, "Ya got no sense of humour!" Well, Newfoundlanders are a famously funny people who enjoy a good joke when they recognize one, but this was pushing it.

Undaunted, Ted has vowed that by the year 2000, he will contrive, through blackmail if necessary, to get himself appointed Minister of Culture and Correctional Facilities. He assures me that the second item on his Ministerial agenda, after he brings back public floggings on the Court House steps, will be to call for mandatory balconies in all provincial movie theatres.

We'll need our famous sense of humour then, believe me. If the Right Honourable Ted has anything to do with it, life in Newfoundland will just be a laugh a minute. And going to the movies will be an experience you'll never forget. Look out below!

SOUND: A NAUSEATING "ECCCCHHH!" AND THE LOUD SPLAT!!! OF VOMIT FALLING ON HUMAN HEADS.

For Week-End A. M., I'm Absolutely Frank.

November 1994

"Cousin Ted Roasting on an Open Fire . . ."

One listener was highly offended by my tasteless reference to Bloc Quebecois leader Lucien Bouchard, who had just suffered and survived an attack of the mysterious "flesh-eating" disease. Hey, it was a joke!

"Dear Santa,

My name is either Kimmy or Timmy. I'm not sure which 'cause I was only just born. You've probably guessed by now that my Dad is writing this for me. If you remember me from last year, I wasn't even conceived but my Dad wrote the letter for me then, too, just in case the Miracle of Life happened after the New Year's Eve party.

Now, down to business—I would like a Mighty Morphin Power Rangers Death Ray for Christmas. I would also like an interest-free loan for fifteen or twenty thousand dollars, with an indefinite repayment plan. Also a lifetime Prozac prescription. Please bring my Mom a Lady Remington shaver and a box of chocolate-covered Turtles for my Dad.

I know you must get tired of the same old milk-and-cookies routine every year, so I'll leave a shot of bourbon and a plate of crab puffs for you. Enjoy!

Say hello to Mrs Claus and Rudolph and all the little elves or gnomes or whatever the hell they are.

Love,
Kimmy, Timmy, Tammy or Butch"

Ah, how the times have changed. When my Cousin Ted and I were kids (yes, Virginia, Ted was once a child), we used to write our letters to Santa Claus together—y'know, comparing notes, making sure not to ask for exactly the same things. Then we'd take them down to the basement, toss them into the blazing coal furnace and send them on their way. I'm still not sure where this particular Christmas tradition came from. I suppose the theory was that the letters would somehow magically transport themselves to the North Pole. I have no idea how Santa was supposed to read a pile of ashes. And if millions of other kids were doing the same thing, I expect Santa and his elves would be up to their sleigh bells in soot.

Nonetheless, we'd generally get most of what we asked for. Considering our parents' financial status, this was like the Miracle on Mullock Street. My Christmas wish-list, inspired by the Simpson-Sears and Eaton's catalogues, had a tendency to run to things like farm sets, garages and other forms of real estate. I don't know why. Ted was more inclined to ask for chemistry sets and weapons. Intervention at that point by a qualified child psychologist might have saved us all a lot of trouble, but . . . ah, well. Spilt milk, etc.

In these days of electric heat and oil furnaces, kids seem content to send their "Dear Santa" letters to *The Evening Telegram*, labouring under the illusion that Santa subscribes to The People's Paper. If he does, I wonder what he makes of all those lonely hearts who write in to "The Meeting Place" looking for love, companionship and clean, kinky sex? This worries me. What if he gets the personal ads confused with the "Dear Santa" letters? There'll be quite a few kids getting peculiar surprises in their stockings this Christmas. Not to mention the odd sex-crazed adult who winds up with a Barbie doll instead of something (or someone) more . . . flexible.

But why sully the festive season with such crass meanderings? Christmas is a jolly old time for everyone, even Cousin Ted. I just hope he has sense enough not to try pulling the same scam he used last year. He stationed himself outside Woolworth's with a brass kettle and a tripod, dressed in an old pea-jacket and calling himself "The Salvation Navy." The cops eventually removed him after a scuffle broke out between Ted and a gang of Salvationist thugs. A team of doctors at St. Clare's laboured for hours to remove the kettle from Ted's head . . .

I suppose we'll have to have Ted over for Christmas dinner again this year. My wife Hazel dreads this, since Ted always insists on carving the turkey, and Ted with a large knife in his hand and a skinful of hi-test egg-nog is no laughing matter. Two Christmases ago he misjudged by a foot or so and carved a hearty slice of dark meat out of the cat.

However, 'tis the season for peace on earth and goodwill towards men, even men like Ted or "Gimpy" Bouchard. As sanctimonious politicians are fond of saying, we must put aside our differences at times like these. Maybe Ted and I will re-live our childhood, write our letters to Santa together and toss them into the fireplace. Or . . . maybe I'll just toss Ted into the fireplace . . . hmmm.

Dear Santa, my name is Absolutely Frank. Merry Christmas!

December 1994

Resolution No. 9

John Efford is an unwittingly funny provincial Cabinet Minister.

Well, here we are, a whole week into the New Year. If you're like me, you've already broken most of the resolutions you made after guzzling all that contraband London Dock on New Year's Eve. They all seemed like good ideas at the time—stop smoking, exercise more, eat better, be nicer to people you really can't stand—but, let's face it, the novelty and good intentions wear off pretty darn fast.

Why do we bother making resolutions anyway? I know why I do it—for the sake of my own sanity. I have to at least *pretend* that things might get better this year. I mean, how much worse could they get? *Don't answer that!*

Needless to say, I ran into trouble with my resolutions within minutes of making them. My first resolution was typical: give up smoking. Yeah, sure. Who am I kidding? I've been down that road before and it's an unpaved cul-de-sac. Scratch that one.

Next—at my wife Hazel's prompting, I resolved to stop bitching and complaining about everything. No good—what would I do for a living? Complaining is my livelihood, and I don't dare stop. To live is to complain, that's my motto. Jeez, if I couldn't complain, I'd be a hollow shell of the cranky S.O.B. that I am. So, scratch that one, too.

Let's broaden it out a bit: "I vow to fight for world peace!" Hmm. Naaaah. Let's move on. "I will stop spiking the Confederation Building water coolers with LSD, as it doesn't seem to be having any effect." Although . . . it would explain things like the recent Cabinet shuffle and John Efford.

Well, here's one resolution I can keep—"I will ignore my Cousin Ted." Unfortunately, Cousin Ted is kinda like saturated fat—ignoring him isn't the same thing as eliminating him altogether. Especially when I know for a fact that one of Ted's resolutions is to "get closer to Cousin Frank." Dear God! Ted is already far too close for comfort. If he got any closer, we'd be sharing the same pair of pants.

Cousin Ted's list of New Year's resolutions also includes things like "I will use cutlery at the dinner table!" and "No more crank calls to Clyde Wells using the voice of Joey Smallwood!" To give him his due, Ted does do a wicked imitation of Joey, both before and after the stroke. He calls it his "party piece," and has a whole routine worked out in case anyone ever invites him to a party. (Hmm. Mental note: Resolution No. 8—"Never invite Ted to a party.")

The last resolution on my own list is, coincidentally, the same as Ted's—"I vow never to leave Newfoundland!" Actually, Ted has vowed never to leave the Avalon Peninsula. The Court Order doesn't leave him much choice, but the fact is, Ted is not welcome in Central Newfoundland (or anywhere beyond the Overpass). Another Court Order prevents me from revealing more, but I *can* say that the public hasn't been told the whole story about why the Russians won't land in Gander anymore.

Where was I? Ah yes, Resolution No. 9—"I vow never to leave Newfoundland!" Why this particular resolution? Well, call me loco, call me crazy, call me bwana . . . but I suspect there's a hidden government agenda to force us all off this island for good, to make life here so difficult that we'll all have to go whether we want to or not. How many blameless baypersons have already been squeezed out of their ancestral homes and sent packing? Where are they supposed to go? There's no point in them moving to St. John's or Corner Brook—there's nothing to do there. Besides, the people who already live there have nothing to do, either. How about if we all move to Quebec before their Referendum? Think of it—half a million defiantly unilingual Newfoundlanders roaming the streets of Montreal and screwing up the vote. That oughta wipe the smug smiles off those bloated Separatist kissers once and for all.

You won't see me strolling down *les avenues*, though, 'cause I'm not goin' anywhere. Even though no one cares whether I stay here or not, I'm gonna stand my ground. I will not budge an inch! You see, I have a hidden agenda of my own—to be the only Newfoundlander left in Newfoundland . . . that way, if anything good *does* happen, it'll happen to *me*.

For Week-End A.M., I'm Absolutely Resolute Frank.

January 1995

Low Finance

The banks. I hate 'em. My Cousin Ted hates 'em, too. We have our reasons. Ted hates 'em on principle and because they're all computerized these days. See, it used to be that he could write a rubber cheque on a Friday, knowing full well he wouldn't have the money to cover it until the following Wednesday. Of course, this was before Ted was placed on the National Bad Cheque Blacklist.

But everything is automated now, and you can't even count on human error anymore. The cheques are all processed by computers in Toronto or Halifax, or . . . or . . . Patagonia, for all I know, and that leaves no leeway for someone like Ted, who suffers from a chronic cash-flow problem—namely, he has no cash.

Although it pains me to admit that I have anything in common with Cousin Ted, I have to say that I share his loathing of the banking system. I've had my share of unpleasant encounters with the banks, and I offer this one as typical—I went to my own bank a while ago, a bank I've been dealing with for twenty years, to get a $1,000 loan to fix up my leaky roof. They wouldn't even look at me. I said, "It's only a thousand bucks." The Loan Officer smirked at me and said she could authorize a loan for five thousand bucks, but no less. I said, "I don't want $5,000. I only need $1,000." She said, sorry, but we don't loan anything less than $5,000. I said, "Okay, give me the $5,000 and I'll give $4,000 back the same day." She said, sorry, but that won't do, I'd have to spend all $5,000 on something. I said, "On what?" She said it didn't matter, as long as I spent it all.

I left the bank in a rage. I went to the nearest ATM and withdrew my remaining $40. I went to another bank and opened a new account. I asked them for a $1,000 loan. They said

No. I said, "How about $5,000?" They said No, but they *could* loan me $10,000. I said I could never pay that back, but I could pay back $1,000. They said, Too bad, Frank, it's Ten Grand or nothing. "Fine," I said, and withdrew my $40, which had shrunk to $35 after they deducted their bank charges.

I now keep my money in a sock under my mattress. I don't collect any interest on it, but then again, I don't have to pay a maintenance charge to the Sealy Posturepedic Company.

One of the things I especially hate about banks is their corporate slogans and I think there oughta be some kind of legal action taken against all of them for false advertising. The Royal Bank's slogan says, "We got to be Canada's largest bank . . . one customer at a time." For an accurate picture of how the banks really work, I suggest you fill in the blank in that sentence with the obscene verb of your choice. The Bank of Montreal smugly promises "It *is* possible." Hah! The Toronto-Dominion slogan is "Your Bank. Your Way." Yeah, sure. H. G. Wells said "Advertising is legalized lying" and, buddy, he was right.

What purpose do banks actually serve for people like me, let alone people like Cousin Ted? Damned if I know. I put money in the bank and take it out again. The bank then charges me for this service. What do I get out of it? They seem to be making money off me, but I'm not making money off them. The one that really kills me is that "maintenance charge." These bloodsucking hounds, WHO ONLY MADE A FOUR BILLION DOLLAR PROFIT LAST YEAR, are charging me for the privilege of letting me store my money with them. Where does the "maintenance" come into it? Jeez, I could get a better deal if I gave it to Cousin Ted to hang onto. At least I wouldn't have to pay him to do it. Oh, I might have to beat him with a stick to get it back, but there'd be some satisfaction in that.

Ted called me last night with a brainstorm—he figures we should open our own bank. We could make a pile of money off other people's money without lifting a finger. He said we could call it "The Bank of Ted." His suggestion for our corporate slogan was, "Give us your money and GO TO HELL!"

For Week-End A. M., I'm Absolutely Penniless Frank.

January 1995

Love Potion #10

This was inspired by reports that a vast Asian market for aphrodisiacal seal penises was opening up for Newfoundland. Whoopee.

You may fill in the [BLEEEP!] blanks with the human body excrescence of your choice.

For reasons I don't pretend to understand, my Cousin Ted remains fiercely, even obsessively, loyal to Industry Minister Chuck Furey. Personally, every time I see Chuck I can't help thinking he's the leader of a Romulan invasion . . . but that's another story.

Whenever Chuck shows his cherubic mug on TV promoting yet another wacko economic brainstorm like Iceberg Vodka, Ted gets all buzzed up and starts formulating a new plan to cash in on it. So far, there's been the Labrador Diamond Mining Scam—uh, that should read Scheme—the Argentinean Corned Beef Ranch Scheme, the Toothbrush Bristle Factory Scheme, Making Gum Boots Out of Gum . . . well, the list goes on and on.

Ted has tried unsuccessfully to access every possible government funding agency—ACOA, ENL, the works. Nothing ever comes of his efforts, partly because even Newfoundland civil servants can recognize a crackpot when they see one—well, sometimes—and partly because Ted, being his own worst enemy, usually flies into hysterics every time he's turned down, and starts writing threatening letters to everyone from Clyde Wells to Andy Wells (Ted thinks they're related).

Well, Our Man Chuck is all over the airwaves again with his latest economic strategy—the EDGE. I must confess that every time I hear Chuck say "Let me introduce you to the EDGE," I feel like screaming at the TV: "Jesus, Chuck! Who do you think you're talking to? As if there isn't a Newfoundlander in this province who isn't already living on it or been pushed over it!"

The effect of these ads on Ted has been predictably inflammatory. Then again, Ted watches so much TV so indiscriminately that he frequently confuses it with reality. For example, he still doesn't quite understand that the actor who played Mac Corey on *Another World* really died and that's why he's no longer on the show. Repeated explanations and smacks in the face have been to no avail.

Inspired by his idol Chuck, Ted has come up with a new idea. For reasons I don't even want to understand, Ted has long been interested in aphrodisiacs—y'know, powdered rhinoceros horn, dried seal penises, mashed up dung beetles, that sort of thing—icky items designed to enhance sexual prowess or potency. There seems to be a huge market for this stuff in Asia, although I can't imagine why all those Asian men want to increase their sexual potency. The teeming hordes of the Orient seem to have no trouble propagating, so why would they need artificial stimulants?

Anyway, Ted has kept a sharp eye on all those "business" trips to the mysterious East that Clyde and Chuck and all manner of local entrepreneurs are always going on. God only knows what they're really up to on those little joy rides, but since Newfoundlanders are statistically proven to be the most sexually active Canadians, I expect the $1,000-a-night Hong Kong hookers are doing a booming business.

Ted has no access to seal weenies, so he's decided, based on . . . well, based on nothing, really . . . that an alternative locally produced aphrodisiac might be . . . ground-up [BLEEEP!]. He reasons that if Newfoundlanders are so hyper-sexed, their cast-off [BLEEEP!] must be positively pulsating with potency. Ted figures his plan will bring untold millions of Asian dollars into the Newfoundland economy while providing a tidy income supplement to thousands of former fisheries workers and

Woolco clerks. As a bonus, the [BLEEEP!] can also be used as a nourishing spread on toast, or as mulch.

Ted has been trying to contact the Honourable Chuck for an appointment to discuss this idea, and also to get some of Chuck's own [BLEEEP!] to get the ball rolling, but so far, no luck. A Restraining Order prevents Ted from going to the Confederation Building in person, and the security guards have standing orders to boot him in the [BLEEEP!] on sight. I keep telling Ted he's wasting his time, 'cause the Chuckinator is never there anyway. He's off hunting up investors in Japan or Malaysia or Timbuktu or on the planet Ghisghee or in [BLEEEP!] . . .

For Week-End A.M., I'm Absolutely [BLEEEEEEEEP!] Frank.

February 1995

Those Effin' Mainlanders Again

A true story, from beginning to end. A complaint was lodged by one outraged ex-mainlander over my use of the term "ignorant mainland pig," proving two things: one—the listener wasn't paying close attention; and two —MAINLANDERS GOT NO SENSE OF HUMOUR!!!

Last Saturday night, I'm cagged off on the couch after supper, remote control in hand, performing the traditional male ritual of compulsive channel surfing. As Jerry Seinfeld points out, men don't watch TV to see what's on—they want to see what *else* is on. "No, seen that *(click!)* . . . don't like that *(click!)* . . . can't watch that again . . . *(click!)*." And so on. My wife Hazel doesn't share my enthusiasm for this particular indoor sport, but she's putting up with it—for the moment.

Anyway, I'm flicking around and I happen to pass by that old CBC war-horse, *Front Page Challenge,* a show I couldn't stand thirty years ago and still find stupefyingly boring. We catch a glimpse of our own Mary Walsh, and Hazel says "Stop it, Frank." I know that tone of voice, and my finger, poised in mid-click, relaxes. It turns out we've missed whatever story Mary's representing, but we stay tuned anyway while she answers questions from the show's panel of professional pundits. It all seems harmless enough, and my finger is beginning to twitch, when suddenly, the show's host, Fred Davis, asks Mary if her Newfoundland accent has "softened" over the years.

I see by the look in her eyes that Mary is taken somewhat aback, but she explains, with good grace under the circumstances, that her accent is simply . . . her accent. It is, nonetheless, recognizably a Newfoundland accent. What else could it be?

Hazel and I exchange an uneasy glance. It strikes both of us as an odd question. It's true that most mainlanders like to delude themselves that they don't have accents, but we know better. What I'd like to know is why Jack Webster, who I assume is actually a Canadian, sounds like some senile Scotsman, up to his wattles in heather and haggis? Hoot, mon!

With that minor hurdle out of the way, things might have proceeded smoothly, except that another panelist, one Allan Fotheringham, apparently loses his mind on national TV and remarks that Newfoundland is—and I quote—"the basketcase of Canada, and everyone down there is on welfare." My hackles begin to rise. Hazel stirs in her chair.

Am I easily provoked by this kind of condescending attack? Am I defensive? You bet I am. Alas, we are all too familiar with the way we're perceived by the sophisticates of Upper Canada. How many asinine broadsides in *The Globe and Mail* does it take before the point and the perception are crystal clear? Even stund townies like me can tell when we're being dumped on, and, buddy, it's pretty bloody tiresome.

But back to *Front Page Challenge.* I see by the look in Mary's eyes that now she is reeling in shock and *her* hackles are beginning to rise. Lucky for Mr Fotheringham that she's being televised from Halifax and is not actually present in the Toronto studio, since she looks prepared to fling herself at him and throttle the pompous windbag before he can get another word out.

What is it with clowns like this guy? Do they pull this kind of stunt on purpose, just to get a rise out of us? For my part, I'm more than willing to strike multiple blows for Canadian unity by indiscriminately busting random mainlanders in the nose.

Hazel quietly begins unplugging all the phones in the house and hiding them. She knows that when I'm this ticked off on this particular subject, I have a habit of making abusive phone calls to a variety of 1-800 numbers. But, Jeez, how much more of this do we have to put up with? A few years ago, Hazel and I were visiting some of her relatives in Nova Scotia and some nitwit actually said to us: "Come on, youse guys, do some 'Newfie' talk for us." You see what I mean? *"Do some 'Newfie' talk for us."* I swear, if he hadn't been driving the car at the time, I would have popped him one right then and there.

Hazel was in the back seat, in a perfect position to garrote him with the strap of her purse; instead, with characteristically deceptive sweetness, she said, "Why don't you do some 'mainlander talk' for us?"—knowing full well that that's exactly what the ignorant mainland pig was already doing.

For Week-End A. M., I'm Absolutely Fed-Up Frank.

February 1995

A Vote for Ted is a Vote for . . .

Inspired by the fact that provincial P.C. leader Len Simms had resigned, prompting a leadership race between two candidates, Lynn Verge and Loyola Sullivan, one a fifteen year veteran of provincial politics and the other a dark-horse newcomer. The "fella in a wig and a dress" reference is to actor/writer Greg Malone, who frequently appeared in drag as a member of the CODCO comedy troupe, and who had recently taken on the role of political activist.

Voters, beware—my Cousin Ted has decided to throw his hat into the political ring. He was gonna run for the P.C. leadership, but first of all, he was barred-for-life from the party for impersonating Brian Peckford at a Gay Rights rally; and second, Ted couldn't answer this skill-testing question: Loyola who?

So Ted, like other dreamers and misfits before him, has decided to form his own political party. His campaign slogan is gonna be "A Vote for Ted is a Vote for Ted!" He figures he's got as good a chance as the next guy. "Jeez, Frank," he said to me, "there's a fella startin' his own party who makes his living in a wig and a dress. I'd say I got a shot at it."

Question: Where does Ted stand on the important issues of the day? Answer: Aside. (An old joke, but a good one.)

Actually, he's developed a pretty interesting platform. Ted plans to merge the Departments of Fisheries and Rural Development. He will then resettle every abandoned outport with those 45,000 civil servants who are getting the axe, plus every tenth teenager from St John's and Corner Brook. "We gotta clean up those cities, Frank," he said. "They're only a breeding ground for germs and vandalism." Once the outports are re-resettled, everyone will have to start growing their own fish—in buckets at first, then in bathtubs, and finally in small, roped-off parts of the ocean, which will be declared off-limits to everyone except native-born Newfoundlanders. Mainlanders and other foreigners will be shot on sight, and their private parts sold to the Chinese or whoever wants them.

Ted's idea of reforming the U.I. and Welfare system is stunningly simple: there'll be no U.I. because there won't be any jobs, but everyone can get a Guaranteed Annual Income for life, as long as they promise they'll never leave Newfoundland. Plus, it will be illegal for anyone to make over $50,000 a year. Anyone who does make more than that will be forced to hand over the difference to Ted, preferably in small, unmarked bills.

In a radical move, Ted promises to cut all defense spending. "Whadda we need an army for, Frank? We'll just beef up the Constabulary, and send 'em overseas. They can knock as many heads as they like. At least it'll get 'em off *our* streets."

As far as international relations are concerned, Ted favours much closer ties to the United States, mainly because he's got the hots for Hillary Clinton. "She looks like my kind of woman, Frank," he says. I plan to notify the Secret Service.

Finally, Ted's reaction to the federal budget is: "Budget, shmudget—I can take Paul Martin with one hand tied behind my back. He looks like a sissy-boy to me."

Ted takes things pretty literally, and he's under the impression that there's actually a political ring somewhere, so he's looking for a hat he can throw into it when he finds it. He asked if he could borrow my old fedora. I said, "No way, Ted. I'm not having any hat of mine mixed up in politics." He's torn between a humble, man-of-the-people salt & pepper cap and a Hopalong Cassidy hat he got for Christmas when he was 10. My advice? "The hat, Ted, the hat! Everyone loves a cowboy!"

I was steeling myself to say "No!" to Ted's inevitable next question, when he surprised me by asking my wife Hazel to be his campaign manager. He said, "Sorry, Frank, but she's smarter than you." Even more surprisingly, Hazel said she'd consider it. Well, she's due to be phased out of her job at Corrections Canada anyway. She said, "Look, Frank, if this government really thinks the best way to encourage economic growth is to put another 45,000 people out of work, I'm morally obliged to subvert them any way I can. If I can get Ted elected to office—any office—think of the repercussions! Besides, how much worse off could we be with Ted running the show?"

Well, in twenty years of marriage, I have learned this much: Hazel is always right, so I have no choice but to endorse Ted—in the only way my conscience will allow. I'll stick my head out the back door at midnight, make sure there's no one around, and whisper: "A Vote for Ted is a Vote for . . . *(Pregnant pause as the awful realization hits him)* . . . Ted."

For Week-End A. M., I'm Absolutely Frank.

March 1995

Cap'n Ted, Scourge of the High Seas, Says "Argh!"

Amid the continuing uproar over Spanish overfishing on the Grand Banks, Federal Fisheries Minister Brian Tobin had emerged as a Canadian "hero" for standing up to the foreigners. A hilarious development in the P.C. leadership race was the accusation that some over-zealous Loyola Sullivan partisans had bribed voters on Fogo Island with free fried chicken.

St John's West MP Jean Payne had been accused of fraud, then declared personal bankruptcy and was under investigation by the RCMP for financial shenanigans. Bill Matthews is a particularly ugly Newfoundland politician. Keanu Reeves is, of course, the highly acclaimed movie actor.

My Cousin Ted, in his featherbrained bid to establish his own political party, has decided to change his campaign slogan yet again. Instead of: "A Vote for Ted is a Vote for Ted!" his new slogan will be: "A Vote for Ted is a Vote for Bread!" and Ted promises to give away a slice of 'lassie bread for every vote he gets. Actually, he's kicking himself for not thinking of it sooner. God knows, he's certainly not above the idea of bribery. His only problem is a lack of funds: he can't afford bribery. In fact, he wishes someone would bribe *him*.

Ted *is* considering blackmail as a fundraising idea. His most likely target? Federal MP Jean Payne. "I know a few things about Jean," says Ted. I asked him what, exactly, but Ted said, "The less you know, Frank, the better." Well, he's right about that, but I must say it has occurred to me that declaring personal bankruptcy doesn't seem to have slowed Ms Payne down. It's still a mystery to me how anyone with a nice fat MP's salary and pension plan can declare bankruptcy in the first place. I know if it was me, bankruptcy would mean exactly that.

In the meantime, Ted, who knows a good bandwagon when he sees one, has vowed that, if elected to any office, he will immediately table a motion in the House to change the name of Spaniard's Bay to Tobin's Gut, in honour of his nibs. He's fully prepared to go even further, and re-name the entire province Tobinland.

More alarmingly, he's thinking of chartering a boat and heading out to the Grand Banks himself. "Jeez, Frank," he says, "they're only a bunch of Spaniards. They don't even speak English, for Pete's sake! How hard could it be to put the boots to 'em? They might be able to bounce soccer balls off their heads, but I bet ya they haven't got the guts for a real fight."

If challenging the Spaniards to put up their dukes doesn't work, Ted figures he could kidnap Bill Matthews and offer him as a bribe. "Cripes, Frank," he says, "the guy looks enough like a turbot to fool a Spaniard, and, even gutted and filleted, he could probably feed half a dozen scrawny Spanish families for a week."

I said, "Ted, it won't work. First of all, your knowledge of Spanish is confined to what you've picked up from Speedy Gonzalez cartoons; second, I'd be surprised if you could find your way out the Narrows; and third, what makes you think even the Spaniards could choke down a Newfoundland politician?"

Ted reluctantly agreed that I had a point, but he's still itching to confront those unprincipled Spanish swine. For starters, he threw out all those old bullfight posters he's had on his wall since 1970. He has also vowed never to dance the flamenco again, nor will he ever eat another Spanish omelet. He was gonna start a one-man picket line outside the Casa Grande restaurant until I told him they served Mexican food, not Spanish. "What's the difference?" he said. "I'm not sure, Ted," I said, "but the Mexicans haven't done anything to us yet, so let's just leave them out of it, okay?"

My wife Hazel, Ted's campaign manager, stepped in at that point. "Hold on a minute, Frank," she said. "Why not let Ted go out to the Banks? Think about it: either the Spaniards will be so disgusted at the sight of him that they'll hightail it out of there, or they'll blow him out of the water. Either way, we—and the Newfoundland voting public—win. It's a golden opportunity, Frank!"

I said, "Hazel, are you having second thoughts about Ted's campaign?" Hazel said, "He's out of control, Frank. He's been drinking Diet Cola and reading the New Testament again. He wants to offer himself up as a sacrificial bribe to 'the people': a free snack-pack of Kentucky Fried Ted-parts for every voter!"

Hmm. Maybe Hazel is right. It might solve a lot of problems if Ted were to take on the Spaniards *mano à mano*. I'd phone him up and tell him I'll help pay for the boat, except that he probably hasn't recovered from the disappointment of Oscar-night yet. I know he had his heart set on Keanu Reeves making a clean sweep. . .

Ah well, maybe next year. In the meantime—*Andele! Andele! Vamanos, muchachos!*

Por Week-End A. M., *Yo soy Absolutemente Francisco.*

April 1995

Cousin Ted's Easter Gift to a Grateful Public

Students of Newfoundland's political history will remember Tom Burgess and Hughie Shea from the early 70s, when they created all sorts of interesting trouble.

Well, it's official: my Cousin Ted has withdrawn from politics. He has disbanded his fledgling political party, retired to private life and returned to his first love: substance abuse and surfing the TV channels for anything starring Heather Locklear.

The news will be announced today in a press release by Ted's former campaign manager, my wife Hazel. Well, it's not actually a press release, it's a letter to the Editor of *The Evening Telegram*. In the letter, Hazel says, "I am relieved to report that Cousin Ted has abandoned all pretense of seeking the leadership of his party. He has also abandoned his party. Pressing personal concerns and family obligations have taken precedence over public ambition. Ted says, and I quote: 'Public life has drained me dry. I believe I have a higher calling, and there are more important things for me to do. For starters, it's high time I built that what-not shelf for my Cousin Frank and his lovely wife.' Ted has vowed never to seek political office again as long as other parties continue to put candidates in the field. However, he does leave these final words for his supporters: 'Ask not what your country can do for you. Ask what you can do for me.' Ted will remain incommunicado at his hideaway somewhere on the Witless Bay Barrens until the P.C.s either choose a leader anyone gives a damn about, or hell freezes over—whichever comes first."

The irony of it is that Ted had finally settled on a name for his new party. He was gonna call it the "Abandon Hope, All Ye Who Enter Here Party," and his new motto, echoing the words of Lucifer as he was cast out of heaven, was gonna be "Better to reign in Hell than to serve in Heaven!"—a heck of a campaign slogan for any Newfoundland politician. I told him such classical allusions would be lost on the voters, but Ted stuck to his guns. He said, "I have a sacred duty to educate the public, Frank. If not me, then who? And if not now, then when?"

In private, however, Hazel has revealed to me that Ted was offered an undisclosed amount of cash and some Sobey's food vouchers if he'd just shut up and go away. Hazel was vague on the details, but rumour has it that both the Sullivan and Verge campaign teams finally found a common cause: to exterminate the most annoying political blowfly in the province. I understand that Jean Payne kicked in a few bucks from her private slush-fund as well. It was unanimously agreed that Ted was creating the kind of political havoc that hasn't been seen here since the glory days of Tom Burgess and Hughie Shea. As far as that goes, I know for a fact that Ted, had he actually made it into the House of Assembly, fully intended to cross and re-cross the floor as often as possible, at least until someone called the cops on him.

To be perfectly honest, Ted's decision to cut-and-run couldn't have come at a better time, now that Easter is upon us. For one thing, it means Hazel will have the time to make her Easter dinner specialty, Roast Lamb in Aspic. More to the point, the public will be spared Ted's morbid obsession with this seminal Christian holiday. Ted gets quite overwrought at Easter, not because of the widda bunny wabbits, but because TV gets swamped with irrelevant epics like *The Ten Commandments* and *Spartacus*. "Frank," says Ted, "what the hell have those movies got to do with Easter? I mean, *King of Kings*, I can see; *Ben Hur* or *Barabbas*, no problem. But cripes, just 'cause a movie's got a few Romans in it, or it's some damn-fool Bible story, those network nitwits think it'll do. Well, it won't do, Frank! It just won't do!"

For his political swan song, Ted was planning a one-man performance of The Passion Play. He was gonna carry a home-made cross from the Court House up to Gibbet Hill, where he would then crucify himself. As fate would have it, Ted had to cancel the whole thing when he couldn't get a parade permit from City Hall.

In any event, we can all relax now, especially Hazel. "Frank," she said, "the one thing I didn't anticipate when I told Ted I'd run his campaign was that I would actually have to come in contact with real politicians. I mean, my God . . . Frank Moores touched me! Yuck! I'll never feel clean again."

Hmm. Maybe I'll get her that steel-wool loofah she's been asking for. That oughta scrub the stench of politics out of her skin.

For Week-End A. M., I'm Absolutely Odorless Frank.

April 1995

I Was a Teenage Wasteland

My wife Hazel and I are, uh . . . blessed . . . with two kids, Axel and Donna, both teen-agers. At their specific request (or demand), I rarely mention them on the air. They say they don't want anyone to know I'm their father, which just goes to show you how like a serpent's tooth is an ungrateful child. "Who do ya think pays for your damn skateboards and your Boyz II Men tapes?" I say to them, to no avail. Axel spends most of his free time at a neighbourhood parking lot with his fellow skater-dudes, and Donna might as well pitch a tent at the Avalon Mall. Like most of their kind, they are utterly self-obsessed, and their education seems to consist of what they've picked up from watching Much Music and *The Fresh Prince of Bel Air*.

Their grasp of history, for instance, is sketchy at best. Within the past couple of weeks, the world has observed a couple of big historical anniversaries—the end of World War II in Europe and the Fall of Saigon. These events have made absolutely no impression on Axel or Donna. They're vaguely familiar with the name "Adolph Hitler," but they have the idea that he was, and I quote, "a bad guy, the King of Russia or something." And "Vietnam" is simply a Hollywood set where some war movies are filmed.

If I'm making them sound like "typical teenagers," if I've lumped them into a categorical cliché, well, I'm sorry, but I can't help it. Certain aspects of their behaviour *are* typical, and damn it all, kids, I can't help that, either. That's life. I was a "typical teenager" in my day, too, I assure you. I too was totally self-absorbed. I too considered my doddering parents (who, I believe, were in their 50s at the time) hopelessly out of touch with the reality of my fascinating life.

I have to keep reminding myself, with varying degrees of

success, of what it was like to be a teenager. All in all, I can't say I enjoyed it a whole lot. Oh sure, rock & roll was always a comfort and an inspiration, and I formed a few lasting friendships—but there were also horrors like the stupefying boredom of high school, the crushing humiliation of acne, the terrifying mystery of sex. Adolescence is a minefield that you cross blindfolded at midnight, and I'd rather have my toenails torn out with red-hot pliers than go through anything like it again.

The teenager's lot has never been an easy one, though. It's damn hard trying to forge a personality of your own when every authority figure in sight is doing everything possible to make you conform to some arbitrary standard of "adult" behaviour.

I feel for you, kids, I really do. On the other hand . . . look what you've reduced me to: "Does your room *have* to look like tornado wreckage? Do you *ever* think of lifting a finger around here? Cripes! Wash a dish once in a while! Turn off a light now and then! Hang up a towel! What am I, your servant? You'll eat that supper and you'll *like* it! What the hell do you *do* at the Mall all the time? Turn that down! Are you deaf or what? Do your homework *now!* Get off the phone! *Get off the phone!* Ten bucks!? For what?"

Oh my God, it's depressing to hear myself saying stuff like that. And it only gets worse: "You think *you've* got it hard? Wait till it's *your* turn to be a parent. If I'm hard on you, it's for your own good. Don't smoke! *(Cough, hack)* Don't drink! *(Glug, glug)* Act your age! Grow up!" And then there's the real clincher: "Whadda you have to say for yourself?"

And that, of course, is a question to which there is only one acceptable teenage reply: "A A A R R R R G G G H H H ! ! ! ! !"

You're bombarded with so many conflicting messages as a teenager, it's a wonder anyone survives it. I keep telling Axel and Donna, "Listen, I know what you're going through—I've been there." They don't believe me, of course. Why should they? I'm just Dad, the Old Man (I'm only 46!). I take some small and mean-spirited comfort from the fact that they don't get along any better with Hazel, who has adopted *"Because I say so!"* as her theme song.

What especially worries me is that they've gotten real chummy with my Cousin Ted lately. "He's so cool," they say. "He doesn't order us around all the time, he just lets us hang out." And then they smugly hurl the final insult: "Why can't you and Mom be more like Uncle Ted?"

For Week-End A.M., I'm Absolutely A A R R G G H H!!!

May 1995

PART THREE

Carry That Weight

Frank suffers the tortures of the damned, loses his mind briefly, receives an ultimatum and spends time in The Dark Ward; Hazel takes an active role in Frank's rehabilitation; Cousin Ted only makes matters worse.

A Report from the Front Lines

This piece signaled a radical shift in tone and style—up to now, the Franks had been written as monologues, and this was the first time I wrote a continuous dialogue between Frank and Cousin Ted. Then, as afterwards, I performed both voices. (Frank's voice is as normal as my own, while Ted speaks in a nasal, semi-guttural, East End townie whine.)

From this point on, the Franks became an on-going, "real time" radio serial; previously, Frank had merely reported what Cousin Ted and Hazel had said, but for the remaining episodes Ted and Hazel spoke for themselves and occasionally threatened to take over the show.

In June of 1995, after months of futile negotiations with the Churches (and way too many years of rigid denominational education), Premier Clyde Wells announced a provincial referendum to determine the public will on the subject. The battle lines were drawn.

Triton Airlines *was a private company that had been trying unsuccessfully to start a new airline service in Newfoundland.*

SOUND: BOMBS EXPLODING, GUNS FIRING, BULLETS WHINING, THE SCREAMS OF THE WOUNDED ESTABLISH AND CONTINUE UNDER.

FRANK: Mayday! Mayday! Red Dog One to Great Auk Leader! Can anyone hear me? It's me, Frank! I'm trapped in the Basilica clock tower with my Cousin Ted! This may be my last contact with the outside world! *Can anyone hear me?*

SOUND: RAPID BURST OF AUTOMATIC WEAPON FIRE.

TED: Jeez, Frank, shut up for a minute, will ya? Hand me another ammo clip. I can see some fellas down there, hidin' behind Mercy Convent. I can't tell if they're government troops or Pentecostals . . . either way, they're gonna eat hot lead for brunch!

FRANK: Here you go, Ted. Keep your head down!

SOUND: ANOTHER BURST OF AUTOMATIC WEAPON FIRE.

FRANK: While the bombs fall and the bullets fly, I've only got a few minutes to get this on the record so future generations (or visiting aliens) will know what happened here. Let history remember that *I warned the government.* "Clyde," I said, "blood will flow in the streets if you force the Churches to give up their stranglehold on Newfoundland education. It'll only be a matter of time before extremist fanatics in the Knights of Columbus rise up in righteous fury." Sure enough, they came swarming out of their secret bunker on St Clare Avenue, armed to the teeth with unregistered assault rifles and bottles of deadly Holy Water.

In a terse communiqué, Field Commander Jimmy "the Archbishop" MacDonald said, "The Roman Catholic Church is the One, Holy, Catholic and Apostolic Church, and any assault upon it is the work of Satan! Mr Wells, reap the consequences of your godless act! Let the blood be on your hands!" In a historic move, the Catholics and the Pentecostals signed a Mutual Non-Aggression Pact and orchestrated a daring daylight raid on the Delta Hotel, where they kidnapped Education Minister Chris Decker. Ironically, Mr Decker was in the middle of extolling the virtues of "a peaceful and law-abiding Newfoundland" to a convention of mainland tourism industry officials. When the Premier refused to bow to ransom demands, Mr Decker was viciously pushed around a bit and released. "It was hell," he said later. The mainlanders were given vouchers for communion at the church of their choice and a picture of St Margaret Mary Alacoque, the inventor of barbed wire.

Faced with bloody insurrection, the Premier called out the Royal Newfoundland Regiment and ordered that the Constabulary be issued weapons. Within minutes, renegade Catholic cops began shooting indiscriminately at each other and then at jeering civilians. After a pitched battle—more of a free-for-all, really—on the former Mount Cashel grounds, the Pentecostals reneged on the Non-Aggression Pact and stormed the Basilica parking lot, where they were repulsed by a handful of elderly Presentation nuns. Hey, who wouldn't be?

As the situation deteriorated, I urged my family to flee. "Get out, Hazel," I said, "get out while you can, and take the kids with you. Thank God we never had them baptized—Axel and Donna are non-denominational in the eyes of Church and State, but why take chances? This thing is getting out of hand, and God only knows where it'll end." Hazel got them all on the last flight out of St John's, offered by Triton Airlines in a desperate bid to finally get their business going.

I turned on the radio just as a Pentecostal spokesperson was issuing some sort of ultimatum. As she was speaking in tongues, it was impossible to know what she wanted. Just then, Ted turned up at the back door, wearing his home-made SWAT Team outfit and bristling with unregistered weapons. "Come on, Frank," he said, "it's just you and me now. Let's find ourselves a strategic position and defend it to the death." After dodging across the St Bon's No Man's Land, we ended up here on top of the Basilica. Hey, you know what? I can see my house from here!

SOUND: BOOTED FEET RUNNING UP WOODEN STAIRS.

TED: Here they come, Frank! Step aside and gimme a clear field of fire!

FRANK: Oh cripes, this is it! If anyone can hear me, tell Hazel and the kids that I went down fighting! I don't know if it's ignorant, illiterate Protestants or ignorant, illiterate Catholics coming up those stairs, but I can tell you this much—if I get out of here alive, I'm converting to Buddhism . . .

Reporting from the Front Lines of the Great Education War, for Week-End A.M., I'm Absolutely Fra —

SOUND: FRANK IS CUT OFF BY GUNFIRE MIXED WITH THE INSPIRING STRAINS OF "ONWARD CHRISTIAN SOLDIERS."

June 1995

The Ted Zone

The Monitor *is the official publication of the Roman Catholic archdiocese of the Basilica of St John the Baptist. "The immortal Pilk" refers to Henry Pilk, the fictional author of the play* Pilk's Madhouse *by English actor/writer Ken Campbell.*

SOUND: GUN FIRE MIXED WITH "ONWARD CHRISTIAN SOLDIERS" FADES QUICKLY INTO THE THEME FROM "MORNINGSIDE," WHICH IS ABRUPTLY SWITCHED OFF.

TED: Frank! Frank! Snap out of it! It's me, Ted! Jeez, he's out like a light. Well, I guess I got no choice. Sorry, Frank, this is gonna hurt you more than it hurts me.

SOUND: A RESOUNDING SLAP IN THE FACE.

FRANK: Ow!

TED: Sorry, Frank.

FRANK: *(A little dazed)* Jesus, Ted! What'd you do that for? What's goin' on? Where am I?

TED: You were out of it, Frank. How long've you been out here in the back yard, anyway?

FRANK: The back yard? I . . . my God, I must have fallen asleep.

TED: What, listenin' to Gzowski? That don't surprise me.

FRANK: It seemed so real . . . it was the Education War, we were stuck in the Basilica tower, we were being attacked by Pentecostals . . .

TED: Yeah, yeah, great, Frank. Listen, I gotta talk to ya. Has anybody been . . . y'know, askin' about me?

FRANK: Like who? Who's after you now, Ted?

TED: I think it's the Welfare Cops, Frank.

FRANK: The Welfare Cops? But they've been after you before and you've always managed to skeet your way out of it. Why is this time any different?

TED: They're really crackin' down this time, Frank. Corruption inside the department, internal investigations, the works. My "mole" at Social Services is really feelin' the heat . . . someone's been dippin' into the till up there and she's afraid they're gonna come after her.

FRANK: Her?

TED: Yeah, she's a doll, Frank, you oughta meet her. You'd like her.

FRANK: Ted . . . don't you ever learn? Didn't that Breach of Promise charge teach you anything?

TED: That was a simple misunderstanding, Frank. I never made any promises to that woman.

FRANK: You pretended to marry her, Ted!

TED: It was all in fun, Frank. I thought she had a better sense of humour than that. It just goes to show . . . ya think ya know someone . . .

FRANK: Look, Ted . . . this "mole" of yours . . . what're her chances?

TED: Not good, Frank. Like I said, Ruby's a doll, but the truth is, she *has* been skimmin' a bit off the top.

FRANK: What's her job there?

TED: That's the irony of the whole situation, see . . .

FRANK: Well?

TED: You'll get a kick outta this, Frank . . .

FRANK: *Well?*

TED: Uh . . . she's a Welfare Cop herself.

FRANK: Oh, great. That's . . . just . . . great.

TED: *(Proudly)* Yeah, she's my Mount Pearl Mata Hari.

FRANK: Well, what do you want *me* to do about it, Ted?

TED: Well, nothin', actually . . . but I was hopin' maybe you could get Hazel to make a few . . . uh . . . discreet inquiries, see which way the Welfare wind is blowin'. I know Hazel's got connections ... all those years with Corrections Canada and all that . . .

FRANK: Are you nuts? Do you seriously expect me to ask Hazel to start snooping around at Social Services?

TED: Sure, why not? I think she only pretends she can't stand me, Frank. It's kinda like a game between us.

FRANK: No, it's not, Ted.

TED: Well, whatever. Can I count on you, cuz? C'mon, Frank, you owe me.

FRANK: What do you mean, I "owe" you?

TED: Hey, who saved you from the Pentecostals in the Basilica clock tower?

FRANK: What are you talking about? That was just a dream!

TED: Was it, now? Are you sure about that, Frank?

FRANK: *(Confused)* Of course it was a dream . . . wasn't it?

TED: Maybe . . . but tell me this, Frank—why are you still carrying that blood-soaked copy of *The Monitor* in your hand?

FRANK: What? Oh my God . . .

TED: In the words of the immortal Pilk—who is real in this hall of mirrors?

FRANK: *(In a panic) What the hell is going on here?*

MUSIC: THEME FROM "THE TWILIGHT ZONE".

TED: We're traveling through another dimension, Frank, a dimension not only of sight and sound but of mind. There's a signpost up ahead. Next stop: The Ted Zone!

FRANK: Hazel? Hazel! Help me! *Help meeeee! (à la "The Fly")*

For Week-End A.M., I'm Absolutely Raftered Frank.

June 1995

Inside the Ted Zone

The Rock Arena was (and still is) a visionary plan to create a new St John's Civic Centre by tunneling directly into the Southside Hills, which comprise the southeastern boundary of St John's Harbour.

MUSIC:	THEME FROM "THE TWILIGHT ZONE".
TED:	We're traveling through another dimension, Frank . . . There's a signpost up ahead. Next stop: The Ted Zone!
FRANK:	Hazel? Hazel! Help me! *Help meeeeee!*
SOUND:	HEAVY, CAVERNOUS ECHO.
TED:	Relax, Frank. You're too tense. Just sit back and enjoy the ride.
FRANK:	Where are we?
TED:	I told you, Frank—we're in The Ted Zone.
FRANK:	We are? But . . . it looks a lot like . . . the real world.
TED:	That's the beauty of it, see, Frank. The Ted Zone isn't really a place, it's more like . . . a state of mind. We're still in Newfoundland, only it's *my* Newfoundland. A *perfect* Newfoundland. The Ted Zone is kinda like . . . Strawberry Fields. Y'know? "Nothing is real, nothing to get hung about."
SOUND:	LOUD SCREAMS THAT TAPER OFF INTO INCOHERENT BABBLING.
FRANK:	*(Startled)* What's that?
TED:	Pay no attention, Frank. That's all the politicians and religious leaders and sports fans. Don't worry—they can't see ya. I had 'em all blindfolded and locked inside the Rock Arena.
FRANK:	The Rock Arena? But that's not even built yet . . .

TED: In the Ted Zone, it's not only built, it's in constant use. I had the entire Southside Hills hollowed out and electrified. I put every public nitwit in the province in there, and every now and then I give 'em a little jolt. Ya wanna make Andy Wells jump? Just press this button on my Bat belt.

FRANK: Uh . . . maybe later. What's that big dome doing on top of the Basilica?

TED: Ya like it? I had the place turned into a mosque and gave it to the Moslems. I put 'em in charge of the school system, too, and believe me, no one drops out anymore—not if they wanna keep both hands. And once a month, I let a few of 'em run amok inside the Rock Arena and slay as many infidels as they can catch. So far, the politicians are outlasting the religious leaders—they're slipperier and faster on their feet.

FRANK: What about the sports fans?

TED: Oh, they were the first to go. No stamina, see.

FRANK: Uh huh . . .

SOUND: STREET CAR PASSING BY.

FRANK: Jeez . . . is that a street car?

TED: Yeah, that's part of "The Ted Zone Downtown Development Plan." No cars allowed below Harvey Road. I took all the money the Cabot Corporation was gonna piss away and had the whole downtown reconstructed as an exact replica of St John's in 1924, street cars and all. See? There's Delgado's Fruit Store, and Smallwood's Shoe Store, and there's the Crosbie Hotel . . . Beautiful, wha'? The tourists are nuts about it and we're makin' a bundle off 'em. And just look over here... I tore down City Hall and the Delta Hotel and had New Gower Street completely rebuilt, only better. There's no slums, no unemployment, no welfare, and no welfare cops. No cops at all, in fact. Don't need 'em. In The Ted Zone, all crime is *verboten.*

FRANK: . . . It's what?

TED: Everyone got a job and everyone's happy. Newfoundland never went through Commission of Government, we never joined Confederation, the fishery never collapsed and Joey Smallwood just kept raisin' pigs in Gambo.

FRANK: Wow. I hate to admit it, Ted, but I'm . . . impressed.

TED: Yeah, life is good in The Ted Zone. I come here a lot.

FRANK: Can we . . . can we stay here?

TED: 'Fraid not, Frank. I only bring a few people in, once in a while. If I let everyone in, they'd all wanna stay here. Then The Ted Zone'd be just like the real world, and I can't have that.

FRANK: I see your point. Gee, Ted . . . I never thought it'd be like this in The Ted Zone.

TED: I'm a lot deeper than you think, Frank.

FRANK: Yeah, well . . . I guess we'd better go back. Are you coming?

SOUND: LARGE CROWD GATHERING.

TED: Nah, I'm gonna hang around for awhile. I got a public meeting to attend . . . kind of a rally.

FRANK: Oh yeah? What's going on?

TED: Oh, nothin'. Excuse me . . . I gotta get ready. *Auf wiedersehen!*

FRANK: Hey . . . what's with the uniform, Ted?

LOUDSPEAKER VOICE: *Achtung!! Achtung!! Der Ted über alles! Der Ted über alles! Sieg hiel!*

CROWD: *Sieg hiel! Sieg hiel! Sieg hiel!*

FRANK: Oh cripes, I might have known . . . Reporting from The Ted Zone, where, thank God, nothing is real, for Week-End A.M., I'm Absolutely Frank.

CROWD: *Sieg hiel!*

LOUDSPEAKER VOICE: Der Ted!
CROWD: *Sieg hiel!*
LOUDSPEAKER VOICE: *Der Ted!*
CROWD: *Sieg hiel!*
LOUDSPEAKER VOICE: *Der Ted!*
CROWD: *Sieg hiel!*
LOUDSPEAKER VOICE: *Mein Führer! I can valk!*
CROWD: *Sieg hiel!*
LOUDSPEAKER VOICE: *Ach du lieber!*
CROWD: *Sieg hiel!*
SOUND: FADES OUT.

July 1995

Frank Gets an Ultimatum

Producer Jamie Fitzpatrick kindly agreed to appear as himself in this one. He was to make a couple of return appearances later on.

CROWD: *Sieg hiel! Der Ted! Sieg hiel! Der Ted! Sieg hiel! Der Ted—*

SOUND: A PHONE RINGS. THE CROWD NOISE STOPS ABRUPTLY.

FRANK: *(Annoyed)* Jeez, I thought I said "no calls" when I'm working . . .

SOUND: FRANK PICKS UP THE PHONE.

FRANK: Hello?

JAMIE: *(Terse)* Frank? Jamie.

FRANK: Who?

JAMIE: Jamie Fitzpatrick . . . your producer, remember?

FRANK: Oh. Right. Hey! Jamie! Jamerino!

JAMIE: That's "Mr Jamerino" to you. Listen, Frank, just what do you think you're doing?

FRANK: Whaddya mean?

JAMIE: I mean, I hired you to do a little witty commentary about issues of the day, am I right?

FRANK: Well . . . yeah.

JAMIE: Something light and entertaining, not too weird?

FRANK: Yeah . . .

JAMIE: So what's all this foolishness I keep hearing? Catholics and Pentecostals shooting it out, Cousin Ted hijacking the show to "The Ted Zone," Nazi rallies . . . what's all that about, Frank?

FRANK: Hey, I really was in The Ted Zone, Jamie, I swear.

JAMIE: Sure you were, Frank. Anyway, we're getting off

the track here. I've been getting a lot of complaints. That's why I called.

FRANK: "Complaints"? Whaddya mean "complaints"? From who?

JAMIE: From "whom," Frank. And that's another thing ... I thought I was hiring an educated man, and I've recently been informed by my "mole" at CSIS that you never even finished University.

FRANK: I don't see what that's got to do with it.

JAMIE: It has everything to do with it, Frank! This is the CBC, for God's sake! We're trying to maintain an image! How do you think our listeners are gonna feel when they realize they're being preached to by a . . . a . . . a damn drop-out?

FRANK: Hey, that was twenty-five years ago! I wasn't expelled or anything! I just got fed up with MUN. Is that some kind of federal crime?

JAMIE: You're missing the point, Frank. We've got enough trouble here already—cutbacks, downsizing, accusations of elitism, Clyde Wells nagging—we don't need any more hassles. Especially from people who find out they're being duped by some pretentious townie.

FRANK: Oh c'mon, Jamie, get real. How many people listen to Week-End A. M. anyway?

JAMIE: You're missing the point again, Frank. This is the CBC. It doesn't matter how many people listen. But let me tell you something, buddy—if the {BLEEP!} hits the fan, heads will start rolling, and you can bet your {BLEEP!} mine won't be one of 'em.

FRANK: So . . . what exactly are you saying, Jamie?

JAMIE: I'm saying, do what you were hired to do. Stop trying to be "creative." This is the Weekend Arts

Magazine. We don't like that sort of thing, it's distracting.

FRANK: Are you threatening me, Jamie?

JAMIE: I'm warning you, that's all.

FRANK: Hmm . . . if I promise to be good, do I get a raise?

JAMIE: Sorry, Frank, a budget is a budget. Besides, I'd say you're doing okay for a guy who never even got a degree.

FRANK: Will you stop harping on that? Are you gonna tell me CBC's audience is made up entirely of University graduates?

JAMIE: *(Sighing wistfully)* If only. Look, I gotta go, Frank. Why don't you take a little break for a while? Get some rest. You obviously need it. And remember what I said. Oh, and by the way . . . I'm looking at your contract right now and I don't see your Cousin Ted's name on it anywhere.

FRANK: Meaning?

JAMIE: Meaning, I don't wanna hear your wacko family on the air anymore. This is an Arts Show, not a Freak Show.

SOUND: JAMIE HANGS UP HIS PHONE.

FRANK: Hello? Hello? Jamie? Jamerino? Damn!

SOUND: FRANK HANGS UP.

TED: Who was that, Frank?

FRANK: The producer. He's not happy.

TED: No? Take my advice, Frank—tell him to blow it out his corporate {BLEEP!}.

FRANK: Jesus, Ted! You're the one who got me into this mess! The bloody "Ted Zone," for God's sake! This is all your fault! Why did I ever listen to you? I must've been nuts!

TED: You worry too much, Frank. Take it easy. Listen, where does this Fitzpatrick guy live?

FRANK: I don't know. Why?

TED: Oh, no reason. Just curious . . .

FRANK: Oh no, Ted. Don't you dare! Jamie! Mr Fitzpatrick, sir! Are you listening? I'll be good from now on, I promise! I won't shag around with the format anymore! How's this? *(Calmly and soberly, as befits the CBC)*: "For Week-End A.M., I'm Absolutely Frank."

TED: That sucks, Frank.

FRANK SIGHS A DEFEATED KIND OF SIGH.

July 1995

A Frank Report from the Dark Ward

Dave Gilbert was a Provincial Cabinet Minister recently convicted of fraud.

Gerry Fallon and Earl Batstone were the principal public mouthpieces for, respectively, the Roman Catholic and Pentecostal School Boards during the hotly contested Referendum on Education Reform in Newfoundland.

This was CBC Radio producer Francesca Swann's first appearance as the charmingly English-accented Voice of Hazel.

HAZEL: Testing one-two-three, testing . . . is this on? Okay. Hello, this is Absolutely Hazel? Frank's wife? Frank has been under a lot of strain recently, what with the Bernardo Trial and Dave Gilbert's conviction and his Cousin Ted and the sound of Preston Manning's voice and the Education Referendum and those spitey Quebecois and . . . well, you get the picture. After his last commentary, Frank had a slight . . . uh . . . episode in the studio. Someone mentioned the words "St John's Civic Centre" and . . . well, he snapped and ran amok. Several CBC employees were injured trying to bring him down, but the Corporation was very understanding and no lawsuits are pending.

In the meantime, Frank has asked me to assure his listeners that he's feeling much better now and will be back on the job soon. The medication is beginning to work and his doctors say that, as long as he avoids the television, the radio, the newspapers and his Cousin Ted, he should make a full recovery. Although he is not allowed regular visitors, he did give me a tape that he wants to have played on the air. I said, "Frank, you don't have to explain yourself to anybody," but he insisted, because that's the kind of responsible citizen he is. *(She gets a little weepy.)* Oh, Frank, I'm so proud of you. Here is the tape. *(She sniffs.)*

SOUND: TAPE CASSETTE MACHINE BEING TURNED ON.

FRANK: *(A little shaky)* Hello, everyone. It's me, Absolutely . . . uh, Frank. Let me say right off the bat that I'm being well cared for. It's quiet here in The Dark Ward, except for the damn tapping inside the walls. I like it in here. No one talks to me, and I don't have to talk to anyone if I don't want to. Hazel tells me that everything is going on as usual in the outside world and that scares me. Hazel is my wife. We have some kids and two pets. I miss my pets. They never ask me ridiculous questions. Sometimes I think I'd like to be a dog or a cat or a little budgie bird. What *is* that tapping? Doctor Wu says I shouldn't worry about it, but I *am* worried about it. What if it's rats or politicians or Pentecostals trying to get at me? Doctor Wu says no one can get in here, but *I'm* in here, and *he* gets in here, *so don't tell me no one can get in here, Doctor Wu, if that really is your name!*

Sorry, sorry . . . I'm all right. No need for the hoses. My Cousin Ted tried to visit me but the hospital staff chased him off the grounds. I think he's hiding over in Bowring Park. My room doesn't have a window but I know he's over there. He's wearing jewels and binoculars and riding around the Park on the caribou statue. Me and Ted used to spend a lot of time in Bowring Park when we were kids. Ted used to feed pennies to the swans and flatten frogs on the railway tracks. There were little mice and rats and things on the Peter Pan statue and they scared me. *Stop that racket!*

Summer is over now. I like the summer. I like it here in the Dark Ward. It's warm and quiet and I don't have to think about things that scare me, like the government pushing the retirement age to 69. I'm afraid they'll keep pushing it higher and higher so you won't be eligible for your pension until after you're dead. Lots of things scare me. I'm scared of fundamentalist fruitcakes like Gerry Fallon and Earl Batstone. I'm scared of that wacko who thinks Clyde Wells wears his hair brushed forward to hide the number 666 branded on his forehead. I'm scared of Clyde, too, not because he might be the Anti- Christ but because he's a lawyer. The new Fall TV schedule scares me. Even the Weather Channel scares me. Oh, who am I kidding? Everything scares me. *What's that noise?*

Oh . . . it's okay, they're just locking down the Ward. That's good. I'm gonna give this tape to Hazel so she can get CBC to play it on the air, so everyone will know I'm feeling much better now. Hazel is my wife. I like her. She's warm and quiet.

I'm forgetting something . . . uh . . . I got it! For Week-End A.M., I'm Absolutely . . . uh . . . Frank. Yeah, that's it. Frank. Right . . . is that okay, Hazel?

HAZEL: *(Soothing)* That's just fine, Frank. You lie down again, now. It's time to take your meds . . .

SOUND: TAPE CASSETTE MACHINE CLICKS OFF.

September 1995

I Read the News Today . . . Oh Boy, Oh Boy, Oh Boy

Toni Marie Wiseman, Fred Hutton and Lynn Burry are the anchorpeople on the local NTV Evening News. *Debbie Cooper and Doug Letto are their counterparts on CBC's Evening News show,* Here and Now.

FRANK: I am a self-confessed "news junkie," and I make no apology for it. Call me obsessive, call me compulsive, call me a basket case, call me a fruitcake . . .

HAZEL *(Warning)*Frank . . . ! ?

FRANK: Sorry, hon . . . I just like to know what's going on, whether it's here in St John's or around the world. So I watch the news, I read the news, I hear the news. You might say I'm stuffed full of news, like a big mushroom *hors d'oeuvre*. Doctor Wu thinks I watch too much news, which may partly account for some of the . . . uh . . . difficulties I've had lately.

The biggest problem with the news is that there's so much of it going on all the time. You can't possibly keep up with it all, even if you watch CNN and CBC *Newsworld* till your head falls off. I suppose there was just as much news years ago, but it seemed more . . . I don't know, manageable. I mean, when Don Jamieson used to do *News Cavalcade* on CJON, he didn't need an hour-long show.

CJON, of course, is now . . . *(FRANK drifts a little)* . . . uh, CJON is . . . hey, remember this? *(FRANK hums the* News Cavalcade *theme)* It's the *News*

Cavalcade theme! Gee, it's weird the way some things stick in your head, even after forty years. How about the Sally West song? *(FRANK sings)* "Cream of the West Flour, Always the Best Flour, Always the Best for Your Baking." Or my favourite—the Terra Nova Motors song! *(FRANK sings again)*

"Terra Nova Motors, Terra Nova Motor
(Pontiac, Buick)
Terra Nova Motors
(Vauxhall, GMC Trucks)—Terra Nova!
If you're looking for a used car, my friend
It's Terra Nova Motors we recommend.
Now is the very best time to buy
And here is the man who will tell you why.
Terra Nova Motors, Terra Nova Motors,
Terra Nova . . . "

HAZEL: What are you doing, Frank? Are you rambling again?

FRANK: No, no . . . I just got sidetracked, thinking about CJON. That was before your time, Hazel. Did you like the song?

HAZEL: That was a real song? Well, it was . . . charming. But honestly, Frank, even after twenty years of marriage, you can still manage to surprise me. Have you ever thought of taking up singing as a second career?

FRANK: Well, that's sweet of you, Hazel, but I'd be happy just to have a first career . . .

HAZEL: Right. Silly of me. Carry on.

FRANK: Uh . . . what was I talking about?

HAZEL: The News, Frank, the News. Try to stay on track, darling . . .

FRANK: Oh yeah. A phrase I keep hearing from TV anchorpersons everywhere is "the latest news, weather, sports and much more." Now, what exactly does that mean? There's never "much more," unless they're referring to the commercials. Jeez, until they expanded to an hour, the *NTV Evening News* was barely able to squeeze the actual news into their half-hour format, let alone "much more." By the time they got to the Sky-Scan Weather, they'd usually have run over their time-slot. That's okay, though, 'cause I watch the *NTV News* for one reason only—to see how Toni Marie Wiseman is wearing her hair each night.

CBC's *Here and Now* has recently undergone a face lift of sorts, with new theme music and the dull and tedious Doug Letto replacing the dull and tedious Glenn Tilley. To tell you the truth, I kind of miss the ol' *Glennmeister*. Yes, he was dull as dish-water, but you could depend on him to be dull and he never tried to be, God help us, "entertaining." See, the fashion for TV anchorpeople today is to deliver the news in an engaging manner. That usually means a pair of anchorfolks (preferably a man and a woman with plausible faces and good teeth) making feeble attempts at "repartee" in between news items. This might possibly work if the man and woman in question have any wit to begin with, but unfortunately a sense of humour is not a pre-requisite for being an anchorhuman.

For a while there, I tried to get my ignoramus Cousin Ted to pay attention to the news, to keep up with what's happening in the world. It didn't work. Ted was under the impression that I was urging him to watch "the nudes." When he discovered that Debbie and Doug and Fred and Lynn and Toni Marie were fully dressed, he lost all interest.

Ted might be on to something there, though—buck-naked reporters . . . hmm. Well, anything to keep the public better informed. Stay tuned for The Nude News at Six! Film at Eleven!

HAZEL: *(Sharp)* Frank!

FRANK: Sorry, Hazel.

For Week-End A.M., I'm Absolutely Not-Nude Frank.

October 1995

Referendum!? What Referendum?

The good citizens of Shea Heights (also known as "The Brow") have a reputation for not suffering slurs lightly. No disrespect intended!

SOUND:	TELEPHONE RINGING. FRANK ANSWERS.
FRANK:	*(Suspicious)* Hello?
TED:	Hey, Frank, how's it goin', cuz?
FRANK:	*(Sighing)* What is it this time, Ted?
TED:	*(Hurt)* Jeez, Frank, don't be like that. I swear I'll pay ya back . . .
FRANK:	Yeah, yeah. Listen, if you're not calling about money, then what *do* you want?
TED:	Nothin', Frank, nothin'. I just wanted to put in a good word for poor little Dougie Letto. I heard ya last time, y'know, and I got to take exception.
FRANK:	Not you, too? It was just a joke, Ted . . .
TED:	Tell that to Doug, Frank. I know just by lookin' at him that you hurt his feelings. He got a sensitive face.
FRANK:	For God's sake, Ted . . . it was a joke!
TED:	To you, maybe. You oughta watch out what you say about people on the air. I mean, I heard some of the stuff you said about me, and I don't mind, 'cause we're family and all, y'know, but everybody isn't as *simpatico* as me.
FRANK:	Ted, I've never said anything about you that wasn't true.
TED:	That's not the point, Frank. You're in a position of public trust, y'know, like a . . . a scoutmaster or a bus driver . . . and you got to start takin' that

position more seriously. You don't know who might be out there listenin' to ya . . . I mean, ya know how stund some people are, they'll believe anything they hear. Jeez, sure, if you got on the radio and told people the friggin' Martians were invadin', there'd probably be mass suicide up on The Brow.

FRANK: Hey . . . don't say anything bad about Shea Heights, okay? I think my phone might be tapped, and I don't want any trouble.

TED: Relax, boy, Frank. It's *my* phone that's tapped, remember? Anyways, back to Doug Letto for a minute . . .

FRANK: Oh, drop it, Ted. I didn't mean anything by it. Anyway, Doug can't be all that sensitive, or else he wouldn't be a reporter.

TED: Yeah, I s'pose you're right. After all, it's not like I know the guy or anythin'. Besides, there's somethin' else I wanted to talk to ya about. What say I pop over for a minute?

FRANK: Look, I'm busy, Ted . . . I'm working on a commentary about the Referendum.

TED: The Referendum!? Cripes, Frank, snap out of it! That was months ago. Ya already said yer two cents' worth about that, and I was with ya all the way, remember, buddy? Boot the Churches out of the Schools! Uh, listen, Frank . . . you sure ya spent enough time on The Dark Ward?

FRANK: Jesus, Ted . . . not the Education Referendum—the Quebec Referendum.

TED: Oh. Quebec. What're they referendin' about now? What happened . . . the FLQ blow up another mailbox or somethin'?

FRANK: That was thirty years ago, Ted. I really wish you'd pay more attention to the news. A lot has happened since the Sixties . . .

TED: I know that . . . I remember disco, Frank. *(TED sings)* "That's the way, uh huh uh huh, I likes it, uh huh uh huh." What was that club? Out by the Overpass . . . The Outer Limits! Remember the time we took all those diet pills? What a night!

FRANK: Look, Ted, I really don't have time for this. The country's just been through a major crisis, Jacques Parizeau resigned . . .

TED: Parizeau . . . hmm. Never heard of him. Sounds like a typical sooky Separatist, though. So, what did the Frenchies want this time?

FRANK: Oh, the usual. Their own country.

TED: Their own country!? Cripes, where do they think they're livin' now? On the moon?

FRANK: It's very complicated, Ted.

TED: Yeah, sure it is. I know all about the Quebecois, Frank. They're nothin' but a buncha shopkeepers. Sure, if they got their own country, they'd just try and sell it back to us at twice the price.

HAZEL: Frank? What are you doing on the phone? Who are you talking to? It's not Ted, is it?

FRANK: Uh . . .

HAZEL: Because you know what Doctor Wu said: no telephone and definitely no Ted. Under *any* circumstances. Pass me the phone, please. Ted? Goodbye.

TED: Hey, Hazel, how's it—

SOUND: HAZEL SLAMS THE PHONE DOWN.

HAZEL: Now, finish up, dear, and we'll have a little lie-down. I'll get the coconut oil and give you a nice relaxing massage.

FRANK: Really? Well, in that case . . . Quebec can wait. *(Hurriedly)* For Week-End A.M., I'm Absolutely Frank. Okay, start flexing those fingers, hon . . .

November 1995

Frank and Hazel Interruptus

SOUND: SQUEAKING SPRINGS.

FRANK: Ow! Hurt me, Hazel, hurt me! Hurt me, I'm bad!

HAZEL: Grrrr . . . you have lashed the dormant tigress in my nature into a fury, Frank . . . .take that, you naughty, naughty boy!

SOUND: A PLAYFUL SLAP.

FRANK: Ouch! Jeez, not so hard, Hazel . . .

SOUND: "AVON CALLING" DOORBELL. SQUEAKING STOPS.

HAZEL: What the bloody hell . . . ?

FRANK: Damn! It's probably Ted. He said he might drop over.

HAZEL: Oh, for heaven's sake! Not now, Frank! Get rid of him.

FRANK: Well . . . I'll try. But you know what he's like.

HAZEL: Frank, I'm warning you. If you ever want to ride the lightning again, you'll get rid of him.

FRANK: Consider it done, hon.

SOUND: FRANK OPENS THE DOOR.

TED: Hey, Frankie-boy, whaddya at? Where's Hazel?

FRANK: She's . . . uh . . . she's busy. Look, this isn't a good time, Ted . . .

TED: That's all right, I'll just come in and wait for her. This concerns her, too. Hey, what're ya still in your dressing gown for?

SOUND: TED ENTERS AND CLOSES THE DOOR.

FRANK: Never mind, Ted, I told you . . . what concerns her too?

TED: Patience, Frank, patience. I'd rather talk to the both of ya.

HAZEL: Ow!

TED: Jeez, Hazel! I didn't see ya there. Whaddya doin' on the couch? It's 9:30 in the morning.

HAZEL: Get off me, Ted.

TED: Wha'? Oh. Is that your foot? Sorry. Hey, what's the blanket for? Whaddya, cold?

HAZEL: Hand me that sweater, you oaf.

TED: Here ya go. What's that . . . Nonia? Some nice.

FRANK: What do you want, Ted?

TED: Wha'? Oh yeah. I need, like, a letter of reference or something from you guys.

FRANK: What . . . for a job?

TED: Well, not a job, exactly, more like . . . a calling.

HAZEL: Get to the point and get out, Ted.

TED: Jeez, you're some crooked this morning . . .

FRANK: What is it, Ted?

TED: Well . . . don't laugh, now. I wanna become . . . a Gentleman of the Hebrew Persuasion.

FRANK & HAZEL: *What???*

TED: I wanna convert. I wanna become a Jew. It makes perfect sense! They're smarter and more talented and more successful than anyone else. Besides, y'know, lately I've taken a long hard look at myself in the mirror, and, frankly, I don't like what I see. *(Hazel gives a derisive snort)* You wouldn't know it to look at me, but I've matured, Frank. I gotta face the facts—I screwed up everything I ever tried—politics, acting, the priesthood. It's time for a change. I figure . . . maybe if I was a Jew, I'd do better. I'm gettin' friggin' nowhere as a Catholic.

FRANK: Uh, Ted . . . I think there's more to being Jewish than just —

HAZEL: Look here, Ted — what makes you think you'd be any different simply by converting to Judaism?

TED: I just told ya, Hazel . . . Cripes, I thought you were better informed. Course, I s'pose if you got nothin' better to do than lie around on the couch, starin' at the ceiling all day . . .

HAZEL: Get out, Ted.

TED: Wha'? What'd I say?

HAZEL: GET OUT!!!

TED: All right! Keep yer shirt on! I'm goin'! What about that letter?

FRANK: What do you need a letter from us for?

TED: I dunno, somethin' about consenting to a "brisse." What's that, Frank? Some kind of legal mumbo-jumbo?

FRANK: Uh . . . not exactly . . . I think it means a circumcis—

HAZEL: Never mind, Frank! We'll be glad to write you the letter, Ted.

TED: I knew I could count on you guys. Catch ya later. Ya know, you oughta get dressed, Hazel. What if ya had company? *Shalom!*

SOUND: TED OPENS AND CLOSES THE DOOR AND EXITS.

FRANK: Jeez, Hazel, you can't be serious . . .

HAZEL: What he doesn't know won't hurt him . . . yet. Now . . . where were we? Oh yes . . . Grrr! Take that, you naughty boy!

SOUND: ANOTHER PLAYFUL SLAP.

FRANK: Ow! Hurt me, Hazel, I'm bad! Hurt me! But not too much, now . . .

MUSIC: RAVEL'S "BOLERO" FADES IN AND OUT.

November 1995

Patagonia or Bust!

MUSIC: "DING DONG MERRILY ON HIGH" FROM "MANDOLIN CHRISTMAS" (Dave Panting)

SOUND: HAZEL HUMS MERRILY ALONG.

FRANK: Gee, Hazel . . . December already. Where does the time go? Just this time last year it was . . . December.

TED: Is that s'posed to be funny, Frank? You're a laff riot.

FRANK: Agh! Ted! How'd you get in here?

TED: The basement door was unlocked.

HAZEL: Damn it, Frank, I told you to check all the —

TED: I got a bone to pick with you guys. That was not a nice trick you played on me. I coulda been seriously injured.

FRANK: What are you talking about?

TED: That "brisse" business, Frank. Very funny. I just figured it'd be kinda neat to be Jewish. They were gonna chop off a piece of Little Ted!

HAZEL: Oh, get over it, Ted. It was a harmless joke.

TED: Some joke, Hazel. Ha ha ha. Maybe you think it's funny, but you got nothin' to lose, do ya? Excuse my French, but I'm miffed. However, since this is the season to be jolly, I'm willing to forget the whole nasty business. Just tell me one thing.

FRANK: What is it, Ted?

TED: What're ya havin' for Christmas dinner this year? Is it gonna be the baked ham or the turkey?

FRANK: Uh . . . I don't know. Why?

TED: 'Cause I know where I can get my hands on a dirty big goose, real cheap.

FRANK: A goose . . . ! ?

TED: Yeah, well, it looks like a goose, anyway. Don't worry about it. And I'll supply the eggnog, as usual. I got the recipe perfected this time. There won't be a repeat of last year's . . . ah . . . "incident," I promise ya. Ya won't need the Kaopectate this year.

HAZEL: Actually, Ted, we're . . . we're going away for Christmas this year.

FRANK: *(Surprised)* We are?

HAZEL: Yes, Frank, don't you remember? We're taking Axel and Donna out of school early, and we're all going to . . . to . . . Tasmania for the holidays. We might even stay away for . . . oh, a couple of months.

TED: Tasmania!? Holy cow! This is a dream come true! I'll finally get a chance to meet the Tasmanian Devil!

HAZEL: Uh . . . wait a minute, Ted, you don't understand—

TED: I better beat it home and start packin'. Is it hot in Tasmania? What should I wear? Jeez, I wonder if I still got my old pith helmet . . . ?

HAZEL: Ted! Stop! You're not going with us!

TED: Wha'? I'm not!? But you just said —

HAZEL: I said *we're* going away. Just me and Frank and the kids. Sorry.

TED: *(Crestfallen)* Oh . . . well, then . . . what am I s'posed to do?

HAZEL: You'll just have to fend for yourself this year, Ted. Why don't you call up your friend Ruby at Social Services? I'm sure she'd be happy to . . . ah . . . celebrate with you.

TED: Nah. Ruby flew the coop. She's up in Flin Flon or someplace now. She's on the lam from the Welfare Cops. Hey, ya don't need a house-sitter, do ya?

FRANK & HAZEL: No!

TED: Just kidding! I wouldn't stay here anyway. Your house don't have the right . . . ambiance. Well then . . . *(Bitter)* Have a gay old time in Tasmania. *(Fading)* Don't worry about me. I'll be fine . . .

EXIT TED.

FRANK: *(Cheery)* 'Bye, Ted. Merry Christmas! Hazel . . . are we really going to Tasmania?

HAZEL: Of course not, Frank, don't be ridiculous. We're going to Patagonia! You know how you always thought it was a mythical place, like Atlantis or Timbuktu? Well, I checked in the Atlas and guess what? There really is a Patagonia! And that's where we're going! Merry Christmas, darling.

FRANK: Aw gee, Hazel . . . I only got you a set of Ginsu knives. Hey, what about the kids? Are we taking them with us?

HAZEL: Are you mad? No, I'm sending Axel and Donna to England to stay with my mother. It'll be better than a course in survival training. Now, sign off and start packing.

FRANK: Okey-dokey, hon.
For Week-End A. M., I'm Absolutely Festive Frank.

MUSIC: "DING DONG MERRILY ON HIGH"

FRANK & HAZEL: Merry Christmas, everyone!

FRANK: I wonder how you say that in Patagonian . . . ?

December 1995

In Darkest Patagonia, a Gun is Slowly Cocked

This was written during the 1996 provincial election. Brian Tobin, still riding the wave of his recent "triumph" as Federal Fisheries Minister, swept into office on a high tide of false optimism. Some things never change.

TED: To: Absolutely Frank & Family
Somewhere in Patagonia
Dear Frank: Havin' a wonderful time, wish I was there, ha ha ha. I figure there's prob'ly only one "Absolutely Frank" traipsin' around Patagonia, so this letter's bound to reach ya. Tisk, tisk, Frank, you lied—you didn't go to Tasmania at all. I found out where you really went from your bank. They were gonna call the cops on me at first, but they became very co-operative after I told 'em I was from a Collection Agency, lookin' for that overdue Student Loan money. By the way, Frank, shame on you! Ya shoulda paid that back years ago. Also, I'd advise ya to switch banks. Ya can't trust that crowd—they sold ya out in a minute.

Speakin' of banks—remember that bank card you thought was lost? I found it in yer closet and figured out yer P.I.N. number. It only took me a couple of weeks to run through all the possible combinations, but I finally got it. Pretty smart, wha'? And you always said I had no head for numbers! Hah! Hope ya don't mind, but I needed a bit of extra cash to pay for some ... ah ...

personal expenses. I'd tell ya what exactly (nudge-nudge, wink-wink), but you know the old saying—never put it in writing, ya don't know who's readin' yer mail.

Anyway, I just wanted to let ya know that everything's goin' great back here. There's some kind of election goin' on right now, and ya can't sneak out the door without trippin' over some friggin' politician wavin' a Red Book or a Blue Book or a Colouring Book or a Bank Book. Cripes, there's politicians everywhere, they're sproutin' up like fungus.

Speakin' of fungus . . . we got a brand new Premier now and he's a doozy. He's handin' out money like it was loaves and Valium—millions of dollars, Frank! The ever-present question in my mind is: how can I get my hands on some of that cash? Maybe I should try and get my own Party on the go again . . . the voting public might be ready for me this time. You got any of those "A Vote For Ted Is A Vote For Ted" buttons in yer basement? Never mind, I'll root around down there myself.

But . . . I digress. Y'know, Frank, I think you'd like Mr Tobin. He's our kind of guy. And he's some sharp lookin' since he shaved off that greasy little Mafia mustache! I hear from a reliable source that he donated the mustache to the Newfoundland Museum, and they keep it in a special vault, right next to Frank Moores' old sideburns. You talk about yer National Treasures!

On the domestic front, your house is just fine. I rented it out to the crowd that was makin' that TV show, Gullage's or Gilligan's, whatever it's called. I tried to rent 'em my place, but they said "this is family entertainment," so I let 'em have yours instead. But not to worry, there was only about fifty of 'em trampin' through the place, and they were only there for a couple of weeks. You'd hardly notice the difference. True, they had to take out part of the kitchen wall to get some of their gear inside, but I gave 'em the go-ahead. I always thought you needed the extra space in there anyway—y'know, to create a better "flow." It looks like a million bucks now, except for the exposed wiring. Also, you're prob'ly gonna need some new carpeting and maybe a paint job.

Well, that's all the news that's fit to print, ha ha ha. Don't worry about me, I'm doin' just fine. Say hi to the kids for me. That reminds me—there was a buncha mail from England came for you, with Axel and Donna's names on it. Since I know they're with you, I just threw it all in the garbage. Give my love to Hazel, and tell her that fox fur of hers fits me like a glove.

Your affectionate Cousin, Ted.

FRANK: Dear Ted: Received your letter. Am on my way home. You are a dead man. Hazel bought a gun and there's a bullet with your name on it. You can run but you can't hide. I will find you. No matter where you go, no matter how long it takes, I will find you.

For Week-End A.M., I'm Absolutely Furious Frank.

February 1996

Frank Gets His Full and Fair Share of Ted

The title refers to Brian "Wonder Boy" Tobin's campaign promise that, under his Liberal government, Newfoundland would get its "full and fair share" of benefits. Uh huh.

Jason Crummey was a young, independent candidate in the Provincial Election.

SOUND:	ANGRY FIST POUNDING ON A DOOR. (CONTINUE UNDER.)
FRANK:	Ted! I know you're in there, Ted! Open up! You can't hide from me forever! Ted!!
TED:	*(Muffled)* Ted's not here.
FRANK:	Damn it, Ted, I know that's you. Open up!
TED:	*(Muffled)* I told ya, Ted's not here.
SOUND:	POUNDING STOPS.
FRANK:	Well, who are you?
TED:	*(Muffled)* I'm . . . ah . . . Fred. I'm, uh, lookin' after the place.
FRANK:	Well then, *(Heavily sarcastic)* "Fred," where's Ted?
TED:	*(Muffled)* He's . . . ah . . . he's . . . out campaignin' for . . . Jason Crummey.
FRANK:	Don't give me that. The election's over and Jason lost.
TED:	*(Muffled)* Don't believe everything you read, buddy. Jason's contestin' the results, demandin' a recount. He refuses to accept defeat.
FRANK:	*(Exasperated)* Oh, for the love of . . . Open up!!!
SOUND:	ANGRY FIST POUNDING ON DOOR AGAIN.
TED:	*(Muffled)* Hey, watch it! That's an antique door.

FRANK: No, it's not.

TED: *(Muffled)* Well, it came off an antique house, anyway.

FRANK: Ah ha! How would you know that, "Fred"?

TED: *(Muffled)* Don't change the subject, Frank (damn!) . . . or, uh, whoever you are.

FRANK: You know bloody well who I am.

TED: *(Muffled)* No, I don't. You could be anyone. You could be an impostor. You could be a Liberal. You got any I.D.?

FRANK: No, do you?

TED: *(Muffled)* It's in my other pants.

FRANK: Damn it, Ted, you don't have any other pants! Now open the door!

TED: *(Muffled)* Stop callin' me Ted. And get away out of it, or I'll . . . I'll call the cops on ya.

FRANK: Go ahead. Call the cops. What're you gonna charge me with?

TED: *(Muffled)* Harassing a voter.

FRANK: That's not against the law.

TED: *(Muffled)* It's not?

FRANK: Of course not. Otherwise, every politician in the province'd be in the Pen. Now, for the last time, open this door! I picked up some Patagonian interrogation techniques I'm just dying to try out on you.

SOUND: ANGRY FIST POUNDING ON DOOR UNTIL IT BREAKS INTO SPLINTERS.

FRANK: Gee . . . it really *is* an antique door . . . Ha! I've got you now!

SOUND: A BRIEF SCUFFLE.

TED: Leggo a me, will ya? I told ya, I'm not Ted . . . I'm Fred.

FRANK: Give it up, Ted . . . I'm looking right at you.

TED: Don't believe everything ya see, buddy. As they

say in the Mystic East, Reality is merely an Illusion. I might be a . . . a will o' the wisp, a shape-shifter.

FRANK: I'll shift your shape for you . . .

SOUND: ANOTHER SCUFFLE.

TED: Hands off! Or I'll call my MHA!

FRANK: Your MHA!? You don't even know who your MHA is, do you, Ted?

TED: Fred.

FRANK: Whatever. I'll bet you don't even know what district you're in.

TED: So what? At least I voted. That's more than you did. I was up here doin' my civic duty, while you were cagged off like a Patagonian potentate.

FRANK: So, tell me . . . just out of curiosity . . . who did you vote for?

TED: Great Big Sea.

PAUSE.

FRANK: *(Non-plussed)* . . . Isn't that a band or something?

TED: Jeez, I dunno . . . they were nominated for somethin', so I voted for 'em. Maybe they'll do somethin' about that Great Big Pothole in front of my door. Now leggo a me . . .

FRANK: All right . . . but listen: I want you over to my house tomorrow. You're gonna sand my floors for me and you're gonna re-plaster my kitchen before Hazel comes home and disembowels you.

TED: I'll pass that on to Ted when I sees 'im.

FRANK: You do that . . . "Fred." In the meantime . . . for Week-End A.M., I'm Absolutely . . . "Hank."

TED: *Touché*, Frank.

February 1996

Mister Sandman

In the recent provincial election, Brian Tobin's Liberals had won a resounding victory.

Adding insult to injury, veteran P.C. leader Lynn Verge had not only been trounced in her own riding, she had had to suffer the slings and arrows of the likes of Ed ("Kookie") Byrne and Roger ("the Dodger") Fitzgerald, two P.C. caucus members who, immediately after their party's defeat, went on TV and delivered a spiteful attack on Ms Verge, blaming her for the loss and demanding she resign. In this way, they achieved a new low in provincial political infighting.

SOUND:	HIGH-PITCHED SCREAM OF A FLOOR-SANDING MACHINE. CONTINUE UNDER.
TED:	*(In agony)* For the luvva God, Frank! This is torture! Yer killin' me!
FRANK:	You missed a spot, Ted.
TED:	Jeez, Frank. I did the living room and the front hall. Isn't that enough?
FRANK:	No. You're going to finish that dining room today. Hazel's coming home tomorrow and this place is going to look like a palace.
TED:	Anyone ever tell ya you got a real mean streak in ya, Frank?
FRANK:	Hey . . . you're the one who rented out my house to those TV people, and you're the one who's going to repair all the damage. Or would you like to face Hazel yourself?
TED:	Cripes . . . can I at least take a break for a minute? This friggin' sander weighs a ton. It's not doin' my lower back any good, buddy.

FRANK: Tough. Get back on your knees.

TED: Have a heart, Frank . . .

FRANK: Oh . . . all right. You can have five minutes.

SOUND: SANDING MACHINE SHUTS OFF.

TED: Thanks, Frank. How about a beer?

FRANK: At this hour of the morning?

TED: C'mon, Frank . . . Hazel and the kids aren't here . . . it's a Saturday . . . no one's lookin' . . . it's just you and me . . . two guys on their own . . . live a little, why don't ya?

FRANK: Well . . . I suppose it can't hurt. Ah, what the hell.

SOUND: TWO BEER BOTTLES BEING OPENED. TED TAKES A GREAT BIG GULP.

TED: Aaaahhh . . . the champagne of the common man.

FRANK: It's just beer, Ted.

TED: There's no such thing as "just beer," Frank. Bottoms up!

SOUND: TED GUZZLES BEER.

PAUSE. TED HUMS AIMLESSLY FOR A SECOND, THEN ATTEMPTS "CHIT-CHAT."

TED: Weird winter, wha'?

FRANK: *(Unresponsive)* Mm.

TED: Eeyah . . . some strange . . .
PAUSE.

TED: So, uh . . . what'd ya think of the election?

FRANK: I missed it, remember?

TED: Well, ya didn't miss much. I had to laugh at Kookie Byrne and Roger the Dodger shootin' their mouths off in public like that, though. Serves 'em right if they gets the shaft. They were always a couple o' sooks.

FRANK: You, uh . . . you know them?

TED: Oh, sure. I knows everyone, Frank. I met that crowd when I was tryin' to start the Vote for Ted Party last year. There's nothin' like dippin' yer toes into the political pool for a chance to hob-nob with Newfoundland's best and brightest.

FRANK: "Best and brightest"?

TED: That was a joke, Frank. Yeah . . . I met 'em all, and I'll tell ya . . . I wasn't impressed. The only one I could never get a handle on was Chuck Furey. He's too . . . enigmatic.

FRANK: Yeah, well . . . that's one way of putting it.

TED: You'd be surprised at the people I know, Frank. I make it my business to know people who might come in handy sometime. Yes, boy, I've known 'em all . . . Tom "The Tomcat" Hickey, Ank "The Tank" Murphy, Bill "The Squid" Matthews, Hughie Shea, Bucky King, Silly Willy . . . you name 'em, I knows 'em. I'm like a walkin' encyclopedia of Newfoundland public life . . . sort of a living Book of Newfoundland. Yeah, I knows 'em all, the high and the low. Buddy who jumped over the Prime Minister's fence? I knows him. He was one o' my campaign workers for a while. But I didn't put him up to it, Frank, I swear.

FRANK: Hmph. Okay, break's over, Ted. Let's get back at it.

TED: Take it easy, Frank. What's the rush? This is nice, shootin' the breeze together like this. We haven't done this in years.

FRANK: We've never done it, Ted.

TED: Hey . . . what about the Light and Power Company raisin' their rates? Wouldn't that burn yer bird?

FRANK: Those bloodsuckers! Don't get me started. Come on, Ted, rev up the sander and get to work.

SOUND: SANDING MACHINE STARTS UP. CONTINUE UNDER.

TED: Oh, Jeez, that reminds me . . . this came for ya in the mail while you were in Patagonia.

FRANK: What's this?

SOUND:	ENVELOPE BEING OPENED.
FRANK:	For God's sake . . . it's a cut-off notice from the Light and Power Company! What's the date?
SOUND:	SANDING MACHINE SHUTS DOWN WITH A PITIFUL MOAN.
FRANK:	Oh no . . .
TED:	I guess I shoulda given ya that sooner.
FRANK:	Damn it, Ted . . . you stay here. I'll be right back. I've got to go pay this bill.
SOUND:	FRANK RUNNING FOR THE DOOR.
FRANK:	*(Fading)* For Week-End A.M., I'm Absolutely Powerless Frank!
SOUND:	DOOR SLAMS AS FRANK EXITS.
TED:	You can say that again, buddy. Hmm. Might as well have another beer while I'm waitin' . . .
SOUND:	BEER BOTTLE BEING OPENED, FOLLOWED BY REVOLTING GUZZLING SOUNDS.

March 1996

Welcome Back, Hazel!

Following her (and her party's) election defeat, Lynn Verge left political life and the egregiously boring Loyola Sullivan ascended to the P.C. throne. The B. I. S. is the Benevolent Irish Society, *and* Ches's *is a famous St John's fish-and-chip emporium.*

SOUND: CAR DRIVING (INTERIOR).

HAZEL: God, it's good to be home again.

FRANK: I know what you mean. It's amazing, isn't it? No matter how hard things are here, no matter how desperate you are to get away sometimes . . . it's always a relief to fly in over Signal Hill and touch down at Torbay. Even when the fog is down to the tree-tops and the pilot gets that nervous little catch in his voice, it doesn't matter—all you can think about is setting foot on that nice solid Newfoundland ground. That reminds me—how was your flight?

HAZEL: Oh, it was fine. You just went through an amber light, Frank.

FRANK: Sorry. I can't wait to get you home, that's all.

HAZEL: Just get me there in one piece, please. I didn't fly all the way from Patagonia so I could end up wrapped around a telephone pole on Rennie's Mill Road.

SOUND: CAR HITS A HUGE POTHOLE.

HAZEL: Ow! My God—I'd forgotten what bad shape the streets are in.

FRANK: Well, City Council has more important things on its mind than public safety.

HAZEL: No kidding. Nothing's changed while I was gone, then?

FRANK: Not much. Ah, here we are.

SOUND: CAR SCREECHES TO A HALT. FRANK AND HAZEL GET OUT (TWO CAR DOORS OPEN AND CLOSE) AND WALK TO THE HOUSE.

HAZEL: *(Dubious)* It looks all right from the outside . . .

FRANK: Don't worry, hon. You're in for a pleasant surprise.

SOUND: DOOR OPENS.

TED: Welcome home, Hazel! Whaddya think?

HAZEL: *(Quietly despairing)* Oh, God. *(Pause)* What do I think about what, Ted?

FRANK: Ted, why are you here?

TED: Jeez, Frank, relax. I'm, like, yer own personal Welcome Wagon, Hazel. C'mon in, wait'll ya see the place. Yer gonna love it.

HAZEL: Damn it, Ted, if you've made a mess of my lovely house, I'll . . . *(Pause. Then, HAZEL is pleasantly surprised, even flabbergasted.)* Oh my. The floors—they're beautiful! You can practically see your face in them! And the re-plastering . . . did you do all those exquisite moldings and rosettes, Ted?

TED: With these very hands. Come out in the kitchen.

SOUND: FRANK, HAZEL AND TED WALK TO THE KITCHEN.

HAZEL: Ted . . . this is . . . amazing! These new floor tiles are perfect . . . and you were right—there *is* a better "flow" with that wall gone!

TED: Told ya, Frank.

HAZEL: I never thought I'd hear myself say this, but . . . I'm impressed, Ted. I would never have suspected you had such a flair for interior design.

TED: Yeah, well, I'd consider it as a career if it wasn't so fruity. A man in my position can't afford no gender confusion. But that don't mean I'm not sensitive. I got a feminine side too, y'know.

FRANK: You haven't answered my question, Ted. Why are you here? I was hoping . . . er, I thought you'd still be recovering from Paddy's Day.

TED: Ah, don't talk to me about the Irish, Frank. I'm fed up with the Irish ever since I got barred-for-life from the B.I.S. They got no sense of humour. And besides, my stomach is turnt with that ignorant bog-trotter Sullivan runnin' the P.C.'s. Now *there's* a typical Irish potato-head for ya.

HAZEL: What? You mean Lynn Verge is gone?

TED: Yeah. The P.C.'s finally got their way—it's a regular Boy's Club now. That'll show ya how out of touch they are. Mr Tobin, now, he's more in tune with the times—he got a whole buncha women in his cupboard.

FRANK: Cabinet, Ted, not cupboard.

TED: Whatever. That's exactly what I'd do if I was Premier—get a whole crowd of women in the cupboard with me.

FRANK: Cabinet!!!

TED: Yeah, yeah. I'd block the place with women. I'd have nothin' *but* women in the government.

FRANK: *(Sarcastic)* So you could explore your "feminine side"?

TED: No, no. 'Cause they look nicer and they smell nicer. Who wants to be stuck in a cupboard for four or five years with a buncha ugly, smelly men?

FRANK: Ted, for the last time . . . it's a *cabinet*, not a—

HAZEL: Never mind, Frank. Ted . . . I never thought I'd hear myself say *this* either, but . . . would you like to stay for dinner?

TED: Nah. I gotta get home and start preparin' for the

	Academy Awards show. Keanu Reeves might be up for an Oscar and I wanna be ready.
FRANK:	I don't think he's nominated for anything, Ted.
TED:	Sez you. This might be the year, Frank.
HAZEL:	Nonetheless, I would like to thank you for this beautiful re-decorating job, Ted. Could we ... could we take you out to dinner sometime?
TED:	I'll have to get back to ya on that, Hazel. I dunno if there's a restaurant in town that meets my standards. Well ... *hasta la pasta!*
SOUND:	DOOR OPENS AND CLOSES AS TED LEAVES.
FRANK:	Are you serious, Hazel?
HAZEL:	Oh, why not? Where could Ted want to go? Ches's?
FRANK:	Hmm. Maybe you're right. And he did do a lovely job here ... I guess we owe him something.
HAZEL:	Sign off now, Frank. We have the whole day to ourselves and I'm feeling ... frisky.
FRANK:	Whatever you say, hon. For Week-End A.M., I'm Absolutely Frisky Frank. *(Fading)* Hey, wait'll you see what he's done with the bedroom ...

March 1996

Never Eat Anything Bigger Than Your Head

The title of this piece is stolen from a collection by B. Kliban, who, along with Gary (The Far Side) *Larsen and the great Gahan Wilson, remains among my all-time favourite cartoonists.*

MUSIC:	SOFT RESTAURANT MUZAK ("ISN'T IT ROMANTIC?"). CONTINUE UNDER.
SOUND:	THE DISCREET CLINK OF KNIVES, FORKS AND WINE GLASSES. CONTINUE UNDER.
FRANK:	*(Singing)* "Isn't it romantic . . . dah de dum de dah . . . " *(Nervous)* Well . . . what do you think, hon? Isn't it romantic?
TED:	It's b'yootiful, Frank.
FRANK:	I was talking to Hazel, Ted.
TED:	Oh.
FRANK:	Hazel? Hon?
HAZEL:	*(Terse)* Yes, Frank?
FRANK:	Isn't it romantic?
HAZEL:	*(Still terse)* It's bloody dark, is what it is. Why is it so bloody dark in here, Frank? Are they trying to save on their Light & Power bill? At these prices, you should at least be able to see what you're eating. Or ordering, for that matter. Speaking of which—where's our waiter?
TED:	Hang on, Hazel. I'll sniff 'im out for ya. I gotta go make a deposit at the Tinkle-and-Doody Bank anyway. *(Fading)* Don't order nothin' without me, okay?

PAUSE: MUSIC AND BACKGROUND SOUNDS CONTINUE.

FRANK: *(Singing again)* "Isn't it romantic . . ."

HAZEL: *(Still terse)* Stop that, Frank.

FRANK: Sorry. Just trying to create a mood . . .

HAZEL: Well, don't. This isn't romantic. It's a bloody nightmare.

FRANK: Well, how was I to know Ted'd pick this place? Anyway, it's your fault for offering to take him out for dinner in the first place. I would've just fobbed him off with a dozen beer and a bag of Doritos, he'd have been happy as a clam.

HAZEL: *(Relenting)* You're right, you're right. I don't know what came over me. I was just so surprised at the work he'd done on the house, I lost my head for a moment. And now look where we are—the most expensive restaurant in town. This will break us, Frank. We might have to leave Axel and Donna in England with Mummy until the summer.

FRANK: Hey, there's worse things . . .

HAZEL: Frank!

FRANK: I'm kidding, I'm kidding . . . *(Pause)* This is a nice place, though. I always wondered what it was like here.

VOICE IN BACKGROUND: *(French accent) Zut alors!* Get out of my kitchen! *Imbécile!*

SOUND: DISTANT CRASH OF CROCKERY.

HAZEL: If we went out to dinner more often . . .

FRANK: Let's not start that again, please. You know very well why we don't go out to dinner.

HAZEL: Yes. Because you're cheap, Frank.

FRANK: I am *not* cheap! I'm . . . thrifty.

TED: *(Returning)* Nah, you're cheap, Frank. It's not an attractive trait, buddy.

HAZEL: Did you find the waiter?

TED: Don't worry, I took care of him, he'll be here in a sec. Ya gotta know how to talk to these people. I was havin' a little confab with Chef Pierre back there. He's a bit high-strung for a cook, if ya ask me, but I straightened 'im out. You guys ready to order yet or what?

HAZEL: I suppose. Frank? What are you having?

FRANK: Hmm . . . I was thinking . . . as long as we're here, I might try this Ostrich Tornados Rosini. It's the latest thing, apparently.

TED: Don't do it, Frank. Stick with somethin' a bit more . . . indigenous. Like the Cod au Gratin or the Trinity Bay Trout. Somethin' small. Me now, I got a strict dietary rule—I make it a point never to eat anythin' bigger than my head.

HAZEL: That must rule out quite a lot of meals.

TED: On the other hand, ya wanna be careful about eatin' some of yer smaller lower life forms . . . y'know, yer crab, yer lobster, yer mussels, yer snails, yer sea-slugs . . . all yer basic slime-suckin', bottom-feedin' exoskeletons. Jeez, ya might as well scoop a bowl of soup right outta St John's Harbour.

HAZEL: *(Nauseous)* Eugh. I guess I won't have the Shellfish Surprise after all.

TED: Hm . . . the Easter Special looks good—Bunny Rabbit Fricassee. Or how about the *Agnus Dei* Dinner Plate? Nah. What's this? *Filet de Vache Fou*? Pass. Ah . . . this is more like it. Hey! Hey, buddy! Yeah, you . . . *garçon*. What're ya, on strike or somethin'? Gimme a plate of yer finest *poisson et frites*, will ya? Gravy on the side and don't spare the ketchup. And hop to it—toot sweet, *mon ami*.

HAZEL: *Poisson et frites . . .* ?

FRANK: We take you to the best restaurant in St John's and you order fish and chips? Damn it, Ted, we could've gone to Ches's and saved a fortune . . .

TED: Gimme the wine list, will ya? Ya won't get nothin' like this at Ches's. Let's see, now . . . I think a great big bottle of Pouilly Fume oughta wash this down nicely, wha'? Whaddya say?

FRANK: *(Queasy)* I say . . . we never eat out again.

HAZEL: *(Still nauseous)* I may never *eat* again . . . *(HAZEL makes a small vomiting sound)* . . . damn you, Ted, I used to love seafood, and now all I can see is those mutant sculpins crawling along the bottom of the Harbour . . .

FRANK: *(Making a small vomiting sound of his own)* Me too. For Week-End A.M., I'm Absolutely Gastrophobic *(Vomiting)* Frank.

TED: Or . . . how about this impudent little Chardonnay? *(Fading)* Hey . . . what's wrong with you guys?

SOUND: FRANK AND HAZEL CONTINUE TO MAKE SMALL VOMITING NOISES AS MUSIC AND SOUND FADE OUT.

April 1996

PART FOUR

Hello, Goodbye

Frank's life unravels as one disaster after another overwhelms him; Hazel disappears for several months on a 'round-the-world joyride; Cousin Ted takes the reins of Frank's chaotic life; Hazel comes home with good news and bad news; Frank loses his job and eveything goes *ka-boom!*

Death, Taxes and the Inevitable Ted

In the late 60s and early 70s, The Tudor Inn downtown and the Thompson Student Centre at MUN were the favoured hang-outs for anyone with an interest in controlled substances. Heady days, indeed!

SOUND: PAPERS SHUFFLING, PENCIL SCRATCHING.

FRANK: *(To himself)* Step 2: Calculation of Total Income . . . Employment income before deductions from Box (C) on all T4 slips . . . well, that's easy: diddley-squat. Unemployment Insurance benefits—ha! Are they kidding? I'll never see U.I. again. They ought to take that right off the tax form. Partnership income: limited or non-active partners only . . . I wonder if that means Hazel . . . ? She's pretty active, though. Hmm . . . Step 3: Calculation of Taxable Income . . .

TED: What're ya doin', Frank?

FRANK: *(Startled)* Jesus, Ted! What is it with you? Why are you always sneaking up on me like that?

TED: It's a hobby, Frank.

FRANK: Cripes . . . why don't you try model airplanes or something?

TED: Now, Frank, need I remind you about me and my glue problem? It took me years to get that sticky little monkey off my back.

FRANK: Uh huh. And what about all the other monkeys? You're carrying a regular zoo around with you.

TED: Never trust anyone who got no vices, Frank. What about you and yer Peanut Butter Cup habit? Hah?

FRANK: *(Grudging)* All right, all right. What are you doing here? What do you want?

TED: That hurts, Frank. Why d'ya always assume I want somethin' from ya?

FRANK: Because you always do!

TED: *Au contraire, mi amigo.* Maybe I just enjoy yer company. Maybe I just wanna spend some quality time with my favourite cousin. Ever think of that?

FRANK: No. Look, I'm busy, Ted, I haven't got time for this.

TED: Doin' yer taxes, are ya? Maybe I can help ya out.

FRANK: Right ... when was the last time you filed an Income Tax Return?

TED: Uh . . . lemme see . . . that woulda been around . . . 1972. Right around the time Frank Moores got elected. I gave it up after that—I seen the future and it depressed me. Besides, there was no way I could report my real income.

FRANK: You didn't have a real income in 1972. Or ever, for that matter. Dealing dope and cheating the Welfare system hardly constitutes a job.

TED: I didn't have a real income on paper, no. That don't mean I wasn't rakin' it in back in the Wonder Years. I s'pose I coulda claimed The Tudor Inn or the Thompson Centre as my office . . .

FRANK: Go away, Ted.

TED: C'mon, Frank, I got a good head for numbers. How do ya think I juggle all those Social Services scams? Lemme help ya. Ya can't be any worse off than tryin' to figure this stuff out on yer own.

FRANK: Well ... maybe you're right. Hazel usually does this for me and I just sign it when she's finished.

TED: And, uh . . . where is my favourite cousin-in-law?

FRANK: She went to England to get the kids. They

would've had to fly home by way of Cairo, Singapore and Mexico City—some kind of NAFTA deal Air Canada bought into. It's actually cheaper for her to go over there and bring them back herself.

TED: Jeez, it's cheaper to fly to London than it is to Halifax these days. So much for National Unity. Well, that settles it, then! With Hazel gone, I'm yer only recourse.

FRANK: *(Sighing)* Dear God . . . okay, then. What about this part?

TED: Hmm ... Calculation of Total Non-Refundable Tax Credits ... ah, skip that. Too boring. This is more like it: Amounts Transferred From Spouse. Jeez . . . Hazel made that much money last year?

FRANK: She had a job last year, remember? Until Corrections Canada made her redundant.

TED: I don't know why ya bother to work at all, Frank. If I had a wife makin' that kind of money, I'd never get out of bed.

FRANK: Someone's got to work in this family. Times are tough, Ted, or haven't you noticed? I mean, 11,000 jobs were lost in this province last year . . .

TED: Big deal. I'm after losin' about 11,000 jobs myself over the years. Lemme see yer deductions . . . Ah! Medical Expenses ... there ya go, now, ya can claim all the time ya spent in The Dark Ward, for a start. Not to mention all those drugs they had ya on. And how about Entertainment Expenses?

FRANK: What Entertainment Expenses?

TED: Takin' me out to dinner was pretty entertaining. I was entertained, anyway. Uh, Capital Cost Allowance . . . Enter 1/2 of the amount, if any, by which Column (3) exceeds Column (4) ... that don't make any sense, skip it. I don't know why they can't write these friggin' things in English, this is

	like a third official language. All right, so whatta we got left here . . . Summary of Tax and Credits.
SOUND:	CALCULATOR CLICKING AND WHIRRING CONTINUE UNDER.
TED:	Line 401 minus line 402 . . .
FRANK:	Hey! That's my calculator! I've been looking all over the house for it!
TED:	*(Getting excited as he crunches numbers)* Quiet, Frank, I'm concentratin' . . . Child Tax Credit (attach Schedule 7) . . . add this to that . . . subtract 3% of line 236 . . . carry the 8 . . . add lines 300 to 326 inclusive . . .
SOUND:	CALCULATOR STOPS.
TED:	Uh oh. Bad news, Frank. Looks like ya owe the Feds a bundle.
FRANK:	Let me see that . . . this is nuts! This is more money than I *made* last year! How can I *owe* money when I didn't even get above the Poverty Line???
TED:	That's the price of democracy, Frank. Would ya rather be livin' in Lebanon?
FRANK:	Depends on their tax system. Look, thanks anyway, Ted, but I'm going to wait for Hazel to come home and file a late return. Right now I gotta go . . . somewhere, and do . . . something. For Week-End A.M., I'm Absolutely Non-Refundable Frank.
TED:	Hey, how about this? Death Expenses . . . anybody in the family die lately?
FRANK:	*(Ominous)* Not yet . . . Ted.

April 1996

Spare the Tape and Spoil the Child

There had recently been an inexplicable outbreak of teachers using masking tape (i.e., bondage) as a form of discipline in schools around the Province. Parents were, naturally, upset.

The Ferryland Fire Hall reference relates to the story of Brigus South, which owed the princely sum of $2,000 to Ferryland, and, as a result, was denied (essential, one would think!) fire fighting services from its neighbouring community. This seemed to me a sad reflection of the erosion of community spirit in Newfoundland. Times are, indeed, tough.

TED: Frank? Frank . . . where are ya?

FRANK: In here, Ted.

TED: How's it goin', buddy? I got yer message, what can I do ya for?

FRANK: Ah . . . just step over here for a second, Ted. Sit down in this chair. I want to try a little experiment.

TED: Hey, whaddya doin' . . . ?

SOUND: BRIEF SCUFFLE. MASKING TAPE IS UNROLLED AND TORN INTO STRIPS.

TED: *(Muffled)* Mmmph! Mmmkkk! Rrrmmmph!

FRANK: Take it easy, Ted . . .

TED: *(Muffled)* Mmmkk!! Mmmmph!!!!

FRANK: Hmm . . . Interesting, but not much of a punishment. I wonder why it's suddenly all the rage? Maybe 'cause it doesn't leave any marks . . .

TED: *(Muffled)* MMMMMMPPPPPPHHHHH!!!!!!!!

FRANK: What? Oh . . . hang on, Ted. Let me just take the tape off your mouth.

SOUND: TAPE IS RIPPED OFF TED'S MOUTH.

TED: Aaaaggghhh! Jesus, Frank!! That hurt! What're ya, nuts?

FRANK: I was just curious. With this sudden rash of students being taped to their desks, and having their mouths taped shut, I wanted to see for myself just what effect it has.

TED: Well, it hurts! Ya happy now?

FRANK: It's puzzling, isn't it? Why tape? Who thought of it? Is it just 'cause teachers aren't allowed to give a snotty student a good smack in the head anymore? Or—does it indicate a more serious problem?

TED: Like what? Psycho teachers? Untape my hands, willya?

FRANK: I mean, you remember what it was like when we were going to school. You'd get the strap till your hands were raw, or get a ruler cracked over your knuckles or something. Or Brother French'd lose his temper and throw a math book at your head.

TED: Simpler times, Frank. Brother Rossi used to hold me out the third floor window by the ankles every once in a while. Then again, he was from New York, so I s'pose it coulda been worse. He coulda shot me. Lemme up outta here, now.

FRANK: The funny thing is, it never occurred to us to complain. We just . . . accepted it, like it was normal. We didn't think we *had* any rights. You wouldn't dare complain at home. Mom and Dad automatically assumed that, if the Brothers gave you a smack, you must have deserved it. After all, they were Men of God . . . almost as good as priests.

TED: *(Struggling)* That's pretty funny, all right. Untape my hands, Frank.

FRANK: And you couldn't go to the principal, either. Nipper Nash'd have you begging for mercy in a second. Remember his specialty? He'd make you get up on the platform his desk was on, then he'd grab hold of those little tiny hairs around your ears and make you jump off. Now, that was psychotic, if you ask me. I mean, he had to think about that for a while.

TED: That's fascinating, Frank, and a fine argument for kickin' the churches out of the schools altogether. In the meantime . . .

FRANK: There were a couple of good ones, though, weren't there? "Chinny" Goodland, for instance. He was a good guy, for a Brother.

TED: Yeah, he was a prince. Uh, Frank . . .

FRANK: How did the "Chinny" song go? "Here comes 'Chinny' . . ."

TED: No, no, it was *(TED sings)*:
"Who's that comin' down the street?
Are they shovels or are they feet?
Yaaaaaaaay, 'Chinny'!"

FRANK: Ah, good ol' "Chinny" . . . gee, I can't imagine *him* abusing anybody.

TED: Frank! Are ya gonna get this tape off me or what?

FRANK: Hmm? Oh, the tape . . . let me think about it for a minute.

TED: What's to think about? Lemme outta here! I got things to do!

FRANK: Really? Like what?

TED: I was thinkin' I might go to Ferryland and burn down their Fire Hall . . . y'know, strike a blow for Brigus South.

FRANK: Well, that settles it, then . . . hold still.

SOUND: FRANK RIPS OFF A STRIP OF TAPE AND TAPES TED'S MOUTH. TED STRUGGLES IN HIS CHAIR.

TED: *(Muffled)* Mmmmmmppphhh!!

FRANK: Gotta go, Ted. I'm picking Hazel and the kids up at

	the airport. Their flight from London was re-routed through Lisbon, Johannesburg and Bogota, and they're going to be cranky and tired.
	For Week-End A.M., I'm Absolutely Adhesive Frank. Bye, Ted!
TED:	*(Muffled)* Mmmmkkk!! Mmmmppphh!
SOUND:	TED STRUGGLES IN THE CHAIR AND CURSES THROUGH THE TAPE. FADE.

May 1996

The Language of Opposable Thumbs

"Ingrid" was my very patient and supportive other producer, Ingrid Fraser, who cheerfully agreed to appear as herself.

When this was broadcast, CBC and many of its employees were engaged in contract negotiations, arbitrations and mediations; hence, the constant references to Unions.

FRANK: *(Distracted)* Dialects and accents . . . *(Pause)* . . . dialects and accents . . . ah, Jeez. Sorry, Ingrid. I blew it.

INGRID: *(On intercom)* That's okay, Frank. Just relax and we'll do it again.

FRANK: Relax!? I can't think straight. I'm worried sick about Hazel and the kids. Their flight got re-scheduled again, and the last I heard they were half way to either Honolulu or Miami.

INGRID: *(On intercom)* It's all right, Frank. Take a deep breath and we'll start over. Okay? From the top.

FRANK: Okay. *(FRANK takes a deep breath.)* Aside from our opposable thumbs and car insurance, the only thing that separates us from the lower life forms is language. I've often wondered why people who speak the same language don't all speak it the same way. Or, for that matter, why we don't all speak the same language in the first place.

Dialects and accents only confuse the issue. Even in St John's, for instance, someone who grew up in the East End has a different accent than someone who grew up in the West End . . .

TED: Boring, Frank. Really, really boring

FRANK: Ted! How did you get in here? How'd you get past Security?

TED: Security!? Ya mean Missus down in the lobby? I told her I had a urgent message for ya and she waved me through. She gave me a cookie, too.

FRANK: I've got to put a lock on the studio door . . .

TED: I wouldn't do that if I were you, Frank. Ya gotta get a qualified locksmith for that. What are Unions for?

FRANK: Good question. Now get out. I'm on the air.

TED: And borin' the bejesus outta people, I bet. What're ya complainin' about this time?

FRANK: Language, if you must know.

TED: Language? Ya wanna talk about language? I'll tell ya what's wrong with language—too many short cuts. D.F.O., H.R.D., C.U.P.E., N.A.P.E., N.A.B.E.T., R.R.S.P., R.S.V.P. . . . people are just too lazy to say a whole sentence anymore, the English language is totally debased. Shakespeare would vomit. Whatever happened to phraseology and dialectic? Whatever happened to paraphrase, metaphor, syntax, philology?

FRANK: Ted . . .

TED: Don't stop me now, Frank, I'm on a tautological roll.

FRANK: Damn it, Ted, I'm working here! Get out!

TED: Hey, this was your topic, remember? I'm only tryin' to help. In the words of Marcus Aurelius—

FRANK: Oh no! Not Marcus Aurelius! Listen, you said you had a message for me—is it Hazel? Is she okay?

TED: Hey, what's this thing? Looks expensive.

FRANK: Put that down!

SOUND: LARGE, EXPENSIVE TECHNICAL OBJECT BEING DROPPED.

FRANK: The message, Ted, the message . . .

TED: Wha'? Oh, right . . . Hazel. Yeah, she called and said to tell ya she's havin' problems gettin' a connecting flight from Tokyo to Rangoon.

FRANK: *(Bemused)* Rangoon . . . !?

TED: And she said she got separated from Axel and Donna in Minsk, but not to worry—they'll join up again in Reykjavik or Bombay. In the meantime, don't forget to put the garbage out and change Fluffy's litter. And she said, "Ted, you get down there to CBC and help Frank with his commentary, A.S.A.P."

FRANK: She did not!

TED: Speakin' of which . . . I don't know why everyone's always pickin' on the CBC. Who else'd let someone like *you* on the air?

FRANK: That's it! I've had it! This commentary is over! Do you understand *that* language, Ted? I'm changing the topic.

TED: To what?

FRANK: Uh . . . I don't know . . . City Council. John Efford. Education reform, anything. The budget!

TED: The budget? I'll tell ya all about the budget, *mi amigo.* In two words—S.A.

FRANK: What?

TED: Screwed Again.

FRANK: I'm leaving, Ted. See? I'm going now. I really am. Bye. You're on your own. *(Fading)* Sorry, Ingrid!

SOUND: DOOR SLAMMING.

TED: Sheesh . . . what a grouch. Ah, don't worry, there, uh . . . Ingrid, right? I can handle this. Lemme see . . . what does he usually say? Uh . . . For Week-End A. M., I'm Absolutely Ted. *(Pause)* That don't sound right, do it? *(Pause)* Wow. Look at all this gear. Lucky for me I got the opposable thumbs. Lessee what happens if I turn this knob . . .

SOUND: LOUD SQUEAL OF FEEDBACK AND A SMALL EXPLOSION OF ELECTRICAL EQUIPMENT.

TED: Oops. If anybody from the Technicians' Union is listenin' to this . . . that was Frank's fault.

INGRID: *(On intercom)* Someone call Security . . .

TED: Hey, Ingrid . . . you married or anything? What're ya doin' after work? *(Fading)* Wanna grab a coffee or somethin'? You goin' on strike or what? Got any money?

May 1996

Ted and Fluffy Explore the Paranormal

A large front-end loader seems to have been stolen from the City Depot and had been missing for some time before anyone noticed its absence; hence, the "front-end loader" reference.

TED:	*(Coaxing)* C'mere. C'mere, luh. C'mon, hold still. Now . . . look deep into my eyes. I'm thinkin' of a number between 1 and 7. If ya know the number, just nod yer head, okay? Hold still, will ya!!
FLUFFY:	Mkgnaow!
TED:	Jeez, Fluffy, c'mon! How hard can it be?
FLUFFY:	*Mrkgnaaooww!*
SOUND:	TELEPHONE RINGS. TED ANSWERS IT.
TED:	Hello, you've reached the residence of Absolutely Frank. If ya wanna leave a message, wait for the beep and then blow it out yer —
HAZEL:	*(On phone)* Hello?
TED:	*(Suspicious)* Hello?
HAZEL:	*(On phone)* Hello? Ted? Is that you, Ted?
TED:	Maybe it is and maybe it isn't. Who's callin'?
HAZEL:	*(On phone)* Damn it, Ted, it's me . . . Hazel. Where's Frank?
TED:	How do I know it's really you?
HAZEL:	*(On phone)* You put Frank on, this minute, or I'll come through this phone and disembowel you!
TED:	Hazel! I knew it was you all the time. How are ya?
HAZEL:	*(On phone)* I'm fine, Ted. I want to speak to Frank.
TED:	Frank's . . . uh, busy right now, Hazel. Ya wanna

give me a message and I'll pass it along to him again?

HAZEL: *(On phone)* What do you mean, he's busy? Where is he? What's he doing?

TED: I'd rather not say.

HAZEL: *(On phone—sharp)* Ted!!!!

TED: I don't trust the phone company, Hazel. Everyone knows they're just a tool of the Brain Police.

HAZEL: *(On phone)* Ted . . .

TED: Remember that TV show, "V"? I think Vince Withers is a space alien, myself. If ya tore the face off him, ya'd see the reptilian humanoid he really is...

SOUND: DOOR OPENS.

TED: Uh, I gotta put ya on hold for a minute, Hazel.

HAZEL: *(On phone)* Ted! Don't you dare put me on ho —

SOUND: TED HANGS UP THE PHONE. WITH A LOUD *"MRKGNAOW!"*, FLUFFY SCRAMS OUT THE DOOR.

FRANK: Jesus, Fluffy, take it easy!

SOUND: DOOR CLOSES.

TED: *(Casual)* Hey, Frank.

FRANK: Ted . . . have you been trying to read Fluffy's mind again?

TED: That cat's too high strung, Frank. He oughta be put on some kinda Cat Valium or somethin'. Where ya been?

FRANK: I've been out to the Airport, getting the royal runaround from Air Canada, that's where. They still can't figure out exactly where Hazel and the kids are. They keep getting re-routed and re-scheduled and shunted around from flight to flight . . .

TED: I don't trust Air Canada, Frank. Everyone knows they're just a tool of the Brain Police . . .

FRANK: Don't start with me, Ted. Why's that light blinking on the phone?

TED: Wha'? Oh, right. Hazel's on the horn for ya.

FRANK: WHAAAT?? Give me that!

SOUND: FRANK PICKS UP THE PHONE.

HAZEL: *(On phone—vicious)*—and if that isn't enough, I will personally see to it that you get an electronic surveillance bracelet around your spindly neck! Do you hear me, Ted?

FRANK: Hazel! It's me!

HAZEL: *(On phone)* Frank! Thank God!

FRANK: Where are you?

HAZEL: *(On phone—cheerful)* You'll never guess where I'm calling from, Frank.

FRANK: Hazel . . .

HAZEL: *(On phone)* I'm calling from the airplane, Frank! Isn't this amazing?

FRANK: Hazel, are you okay? Where are the kids? What the hell is going on?

HAZEL: *(On phone)* We're fine, Frank. Axel is on a flight to Rio de Janeiro and Donna is with me. We connected in Stockholm and right now we're somewhere over . . . actually, I'm not quite sure where we are. It looks like either the Pacific Ocean or the Russian Steppes below us. I'll have to ask Raoul.

FRANK: *(Non-plussed)* . . . Raoul!?

HAZEL: *(On phone)* He's our flight attendant, Frank. A lovely man, you'd like him. He's been very helpful.

FRANK: *(Plaintive)* Hazel . . . I miss you.

HAZEL: *(On phone—perfunctory)* And I miss you, too, Frank. *(Cheerful)* But not to worry—they're taking very good care of us, and it's actually rather pleasant up here in the Jet Stream. No problems, no distractions. We've got plenty of food and drinks and they've been running a non-stop Keanu

Reeves Retrospective on the in-flight movie. Tell Ted—he can eat his liver at the thought of it.

FRANK: *(Becoming increasingly desperate)* But Hazel . . . I can't take much more of this on my own. Things are falling apart back here. Ted's trying to communicate with the cat, people are stealing front-end loaders, there's a movie version of *Mission: Impossible* . . .

HAZEL: *(On phone)* You're not making any sense, Frank. Raoul! Yoo hoo! I have to go now, Frank. I'll call again tomorrow or the next day. Toodles! *(Fading)* Oh, Raoul . . . another G-and-T, please . . .

SOUND: DIAL TONE.

FRANK: Hazel? Hello? Hazel??

SOUND: FRANK HANGS UP PHONE.

TED: Y'know, I used to know a guy named Raoul. Raoul O'Toole from Cashin Avenue. He was a case. Good lookin' fella, too . . .

FRANK: Shut up, Ted. I've got to lie down for a while.

TED: You do that, Frank. I'll hold the fort for ya.

FRANK: Fine. For Week-End A.M., I'm Absolutely Frustrated Frank.

TED: Go to bed out of it, Frank, I got everythin' under control. *(Sotto voce)* Fluffy . . . here, puss! Puss puss puss! Whaddya say we play our little telepathy game again . . . Fluffy? *(Fading)* Fluffy . . . puss puss puss puss . . .

June 1996

Are You With Me, Doctor Wu?

The character of "Doctor Wu" was played by my good friend, actor/director Charlie Tomlinson. He happened to be visiting St John's before taking up his new job as Assistant Professor in the Drama Department at the University of Alberta in Edmonton. I decided to utilize his considerable acting skills while he was available.

Oddly enough, no one—not even a visual artist—twigged to Frank's description of his dream, which is actually a description of part of Hieronymous Bosch's The Garden of Earthly Delights.

The title of the piece refers to the chorus of the classic Steely Dan song Katy Lied.

FRANK: *(Distraught)* . . . and Hazel and the kids keep circling the globe on these big airplanes and then Hazel phones me and there's this flight attendant named Raoul and my Cousin Ted is trying mental telepathy on the cat and I tell you, Doctor Wu, I'm starting to come unglued!

DR WU: *(In a cultured British accent—soothing but dispassionate and somewhat bored)* Yes, yes, yes, Frank, but tell me—did you dream last night?

FRANK: Well . . . yes, I did, actually.

DR WU: Mm hm.

FRANK: I was running through a big field full of jagged rocks and there were two people fornicating inside a big clamshell and then they were devoured by giant insects and then I was chased by a huge knife that was being wheeled along on two rotating ears and then I was flying and then I woke up. *(Pause)* What do you think it means?

DR WU: *(Smug)* As you know, Frank, I do not subscribe to the notion that dreams "mean" anything. They are merely the mental equivalent of an idling engine, tick-tick-ticking away like a rumbling Bugatti. Your brain is an organ like any other in the body and, like your liver or your spleen, it continues its mysterious, messy functions even as you sleep.

FRANK: So . . . you don't think the dream has any significance?

DR WU: On the contrary, I think it has a great deal of significance; though not, of course, for the same reasons you do. In Quantitative Relationship Analysis—Q.R.A.—there are many factors to be taken into account before arriving at even a tentative diagnosis. I consider the fact that you chose to *tell* me about your dream to be *highly* significant.

FRANK: In what way?

DR WU: *(With a patronizing chuckle)* Now, now, Frank, *I* ask the questions here. It is sufficient that you have told me of your dream and that I have not pooh-poohed it out of hand.

PAUSE.

FRANK: To be perfectly honest, Doctor Wu, I can't see that this is getting us anywhere.

DR WU: Ah! A significant phrase, Frank—you said "to be perfectly honest." *Are* you being "perfectly honest"?

FRANK: *(Doubtful)* I think so . . .

DR WU: Ah! You said you "think so." Do you "*think* so" or do you "*know* so"?

FRANK: I'm confused . . .

DR WU: Ah! You say you're "confused." *Are* you confused, Frank?

FRANK: Doctor Wu . . .

DR WU: Ah!

FRANK: If you say "Ah!" one more time, I'm gonna belt you one.

DR WU: Good, Frank! Good! Bring your hostility to the surface! Be a man! Stop sniveling about your wife and your children and your cousin and concentrate! Focus! Remember Clausewitz's First Principle—establish a secure base. From there one may proceed to freedom of action.

FRANK: What's that got to do with—?

DR WU: Do not interrupt me! When one has freedom of action, one is master of one's domain. You, too, can be master of your domain, Frank.

FRANK: *(More confused than ever)* Master of my . . . ?

SOUND: DIGITAL WRISTWATCH ALARM BEEPS.

DR WU: Ah! That's all the time we have today, Frank. I'll see you again next week, yes? You toddle along now and think over what we discussed about your irrational resentment of authority figures.

FRANK: But . . .

DR WU: No "buts." You're not my only patient, you know. I have another appointment now, Frank. A fascinating case, actually, but that's none of your business, is it? You go now and think over what we discussed about your irrational need to know everything that's going on. You may use the side door, please. Ta ta!

SOUND: SIDE DOOR OPENS AND SHUTS.

DR WU: *(On intercom)* All clear, Frieda. Send him in.

SOUND: MAIN DOOR OPENS AND SHUTS.

DR WU: Come in, come in. Don't be shy.

TED: How's it hangin' there, Doctor Wu?

DR WU: It is hanging just fine, Theodore, thank you for asking.

TED: Tell me somethin', Doc . . . what kinda psychiatrist are ya, anyway? Are ya a Freudian, a Jungian, an

Adlerian, or what? Are ya into Transactional Analysis, Gestalt Therapy, Primal Therapy, Vitamin Therapy, what? Got any Prozac on ya?

DR WU: Now, Theodore, I've told you before that we use no drugs in Advanced Structural Analysis.

TED: Say, where'd ya get an accent like that with a name like Wu?

DR WU: As it happens, I was educated at Oxford—Balliol, actually—not that it's any of your business. Now then—why don't you tell me about your Cousin Frank?

TED: Well, for starters, he got this irrational resentment of me.

DR WU: Mm hm. Go on.

TED: And I think he's sufferin' from some kinda permanent delusion about bein' on the radio. Every time I talk to him he always cuts me off by sayin' "For Week-End A.M., I'm Absolutely Frank." Whaddya think it means?

DR WU: Now, now, Theodore, *I* ask the questions here. Are you sure those are his exact words? "I'm Absolutely Frank"?

TED: Uh huh.

DR WU: *(Musing)* Hmm. It's worse than I thought. Perhaps the phrase itself has some sort of talismanic effect. *(He tries it out in a sonorous and portentous manner.)* "For Week-End A.M., I'm Absolutely Wu." *(Pause)* Hmm . . . nothing. Perhaps if I tried some Regression Therapy on him . . . ?

TED: Hey, Doc—what's the chances of gettin' some Thorazine? *(Fading)* Can I get some Ritalin off ya? How about a B-12 shot? Got any poppers? Uppers? Downers?

June 1996

It Only Takes Seventeen Muscles to Smile

Producer Jamie Fitzpatrick made a brief cameo appearance as the Voice of the Council Worker.

FRANK:	*(In a daze)* . . . Hazel . . . Doctor Wu . . . Cousin Ted . . . where's my keys? Oh, look . . . they're in my hand.
SOUND:	CAR STARTS UP & BEGINS TO DRIVE AWAY.
TED:	*(In the distance)* Frank! Stop or I'll shoot!
SOUND:	SCREECH OF BRAKES. CAR COMES TO A HALT.
SOUND:	CAR DOOR OPENS AND CLOSES.
TED:	Just kiddin', Frank. Don't mind if I scab a ride off ya, do ya, buddy? Good. *(Pause)* Well? Whaddya waitin' for?
FRANK:	*(In a daze)* . . . What?
TED:	I said, whaddya waitin' for, Frank? Glaciers are movin' faster than you.
FRANK:	*(In a daze)* . . . Uh . . .
TED:	C'mon, buddy! *Vamanos, moochacho! Andele, andele!* Get it in gear! Agitate the gravel!
FRANK:	*(In a daze)* Oh. Right . . .
SOUND:	CAR DRIVES OFF.
TED:	Hi yo, Honda, away! *(TED sings)* "First gear, it's all right/Second gear, hang on tight/Third gear, lean right." *(Pause)* I'd walk, y'know, but who wants to? Watch out for that pothole, Frank. Y'know, I'd get a car myself, but then I'd never get *any* exercise, would I? Walkin's s'posed to be good for the heart, right? If that's the case, I must have a heart like a

friggin' water buffalo, 'cause that's all I ever do is walk. Walk to the store, walk to the Court House, walk to the Brewer's Retail . . . Take a left here, Frank. Portugal Cove Road.

SOUND: CAR HORN BLARES ANGRILY.

TED: *(Yells out car window)* Where'd ya get yer license, ya moron—K Mart? Turn off yer blinker there, Frank. Course, now, if I *was* gonna get a car, I wouldn't get one of these little sardine cans, I'd get a dirty big Buick or somethin'. Somebody runs into ya in one of them, they'll know they been in a accident, right? Right. One of these things, now, they're useless. Ya smack into somethin'—pow! Colour yerself gone, *mi amigo*. Now, the best car I ever had was a regular old VW bug, remember that? Ya couldn't kill it, no matter how hard ya tried. I drove it right off the Manuels Bridge one time, and that little Krautmobile just kept drivin' on down the river. Say what ya like about the Nazis, they knew how to build a car. "Volkswagen" means "the people's car," didya know that, Frank? I hear they're still makin' 'em down in Mexico and Brazil. Y'know, if it wasn't for the language barrier and the flies in the food, I'd move down there just to get one. Get over in the other lane, Frank.

SOUND: SCREECH OF BRAKES, ANOTHER ANGRY HORN BLARE.

TED: *(Yells out car window)* Get a horse, ya cluck! Hang a right here, Frank. Elizabeth Avenue. Now, boot 'er. *(Pause)* All right, then, don't boot 'er. What I can't figure out is, if they can make a Volkswagen in Mexico, why can't they make 'em here? Jeez, they could start up a VW factory down at the Dockyard or out in Marystown someplace. I mean, c'mon—our peons are just as good as their peons, aren't they? What else is Free Trade for? *You* tell *me*. Hey, hook a left onto Carpasian Road, willya? Look out for that Council worker.

COUNCIL WORKER: *(From the street)* Hey, watch it, buddy!

TED: *(Yells out car window)* Get a job, ya fruit!

FRANK: *(In a daze)* There's a . . . car . . . coming, Ted.

TED: Who, Missus in the Chevy? Nah, she'll stop. Trust me. G'wan, you can make it, pull across.

FRANK: *(In a daze)* She's . . . not . . . stopping, Ted.

TED: Yeah, sure she is. Hey, Frank, didya know this was the 100th Anniversary of the Tootsie Roll?

SOUND: SCREECH OF BRAKES, SMASH AND CLANG OF TWO CARS COLLIDING, BITS OF METAL AND GLASS FALLING ON STREET.
PAUSE.

TED: Jeez . . . I thought for sure she'd stop. *(Pause)* Hey, Frank . . . Frank? Are you okay there, Frank? Talk to me, buddy.

FRANK: *(In a daze)* Hazel . . . ? Is that you, Hazel? I had a long talk with Doctor Wu, just like you wanted me to . . .

TED: Doctor Wu!? Jeez, you talk about yer synchronicity. That's where I was just comin' from when ya picked me up. *I* had a long talk with Doctor Wu, too. Mostly about . . . you. Pretty funny, wha'? He said you were nuts. Then I said *he* was nuts. Then he threw the I Ching at me.

FRANK: *(In a daze)* . . . Doctor Wu . . . ?

TED: Now what was it he was tellin' me . . . ? Somethin' about that thing you always say . . . oh yeah, right. He said there might be some kinda . . . magical power in it or somethin'. Try it out for me, Frank. Lessee if it perks ya up. C'mon, say it—ya'll feel better.

FRANK: *(In a daze)* You mean . . . For Week-End A.M., I'm Absolutely . . . *(With a strangled gasp)* . . . Frank?

TED: Yeah, that's it. Hmm. It don't seem to be doin' that much for ya. *(Yells out car window)* Hey, Missus! Yeah, you—in the Chevy! Ya got a car-phone in there with ya? Dial 411, will ya?*(Fading)* C'mon, ya big cry-baby, I got a injured cousin here . . . whaddya talkin' about, you don't need the Jaws of Life . . . Get a grip . . . Hey, Frank, didya know it takes forty-three muscles to frown and only seventeen to smile? How about that . . . ?

SOUND: SIRENS ARE HEARD IN THE DISTANCE.

June 1996

. . . And Hold the Rat!

CBC Associate Producer Suzanne Woolridge provided the slightly loony Hospital Loudspeaker Voice.

Cousin Ted's description of Doctor Wu's surgical procedure is liberally adapted from an old Mad Magazine *parody.*

SOUND: HOSPITAL EQUIPMENT (HEART MONITOR, INTRAVENOUS, ETC.) BEEPING AND DRIPPING AWAY. ESTABLISH AND CONTINUE UNDER.

LOUDSPEAKER VOICE: *(In background)* Dr Spritzer to the ER. Dr Spritzer to the ER, Stat. Oops, wait a minute. Dr Spritzer to the *OR*, Dr Spritzer to the *OR*, Stat.

TED: Frank? Psst! Frank! Wake up, buddy.

FRANK: *(Foggy)* Huh? Wha' . . . ?

TED: Wake up out of it. They're takin' lunch orders in a minute. Whaddya want?

FRANK: *(Foggy)* . . . Lunch? Where am I?

TED: Hospital, Frank. Whaddya want for lunch? That little Nurse Quimby's on duty today. Lemme order for ya, she'll get ya anythin' ya want. I think she likes me.

FRANK: *(Foggy)* The hospital? What . . . what happened?

TED: Ya racked up yer car, remember? Then ya went out like a light. It was touch and go, there, Frank. I hadda give ya the Kiss of Life until the ambulance came.

FRANK: *(Coming out of it in a hurry)* You what?

TED: The Kiss of Life, Frank. I saved yer life. Remember that the next time I need a favour off ya. If it wasn't for me, ya'd be worm food by now.

FRANK: Oh. Well . . . thanks, Ted. I guess.

LOUDSPEAKER VOICE: *(In background)* Would the owner of the Mercedes-Benz, license number DOC 111, please remove your vehicle from the Emergency Entrance, Stat?

TED: By the way, I never knew ya had such soft lips. Not bad, Frank. Except for the blood and snot all over yer face and the fact that we're cousins, I was almost . . . y'know . . . turned on.

FRANK: I, uh . . . I don't know what to say, Ted.

TED: *De nada, mi amigo.* Virtue is its own reward, right? And besides, like I said, ya owe me. Not that I'd take advantage of a guy in your condition, now, but . . . just keep it in mind.

FRANK: How . . . how badly am I hurt?

TED: Nothin' to worry about, Frank. Couple of broken limbs here and there, a few fractured ribs, a few ruptured organs, a bit of internal bleeding, some concussion, bit of this, bit of that.

FRANK: Oh. Good. How about you, Ted? Did you get hurt?

TED: Nah, just a couple of bruises where I fell on top of ya. That's how ya got all banged up, see, me fallin' on ya. Funny, wha'? Who got the luck of the Irish in this family?

FRANK: Yeah . . . *(Pause)* . . . Ted . . . how come there's no other patients on this Ward? Jeez, there's not even any other beds!

TED: Ya were lucky there, Frank. Ya got the last bed available before they shut down this whole wing for good. They sold all the other beds to pay for some new piece of gear, a Multiphasic Enucleation Veeblefetzer. Florence . . . er, Nurse Quimby was tellin' me all about it last night while we were, uh . . . playin' Parcheesi. It's the latest thing in Liposuction Technology—it boils the fat right off ya and renders it down into suet on the spot. I tell ya, we're on the cutting edge of medical technology here, Frank. It makes ya proud to be a Tobinlander.

LOUDSPEAKER VOICE: *(In background)* Attention, Radiology Lab. In future, don't forget to turn the Laser *off* when you're not using it. I repeat, don't forget to turn the Laser *off* when you're not using it.

FRANK: So . . . did they have to operate on me at all?

TED: Oh, yeah, but it was a piece of cake. Dr Wu came in and did the operation himself. Y'know, I never knew he was a psychiatrist *and* a surgeon. He wrote the whole procedure down for me.

SOUND: TED UNFOLDS A PIECE OF PAPER.

TED: *(Reading)* "First, I will make a incision. The incision is widened and clamped with hemostats, exposing the subcutaneous tissue, which is then retracted, exposing the curved membrane beneath. Next, I will grip the membrane cap with a pair of forceps and lift it with a half turn to the right. I will then insert a Hibbs retractor and remove the gasket with a Stanley screwdriver. Thus, the removal of the carbon-encrusted cylinder-head is a simple matter. It's the accumulation of unburnt carbon deposits on the piston head that causes engine knock." *(Pause)* Cripes, where'd he get his medical degree, Popular Mechanics?

LOUDSPEAKER VOICE: *(In background)* Attention. Attention. We need two strong men at the Front Desk, Stat. Doctor Wu is loose again. I repeat, Doctor Wu is loose again. Use extreme caution.

FRANK: *What did she say???*

TED: Uh, never mind that now, Frank, it's lunch time, here comes Florence. They're savin' so much money by not lettin' poor people in here, they can finally afford a first-class menu. *(Fading)* Hey!

Nurse Quimby! One ratatouille—hold the rat! That's a joke, Frank . . . Frank? Jeez, he fainted . . .

LOUDSPEAKER VOICE: *(In background)* I love saying "Stat."

July 1996

First, the Good News . . .

SOUND: PHONE RINGING. JAMIE ANSWERS IT.

JAMIE: *(On phone)* Studio A. Talk to me.

TED: How's it goin'? I'm lookin' for a "Jimmy Fitz." Are you him?

JAMIE: *(On phone)* Who is this?

TED: Never mind who this is, who's *this?*

JAMIE: *(On phone—amused)* All right, come on . . . is that you, Mack? Ingrid?

TED: Guess again, *compadre.*

JAMIE: *(On phone)* If this is some kind of joke, it's not funny. I'm busy up here, I haven't got time for this. I'm expecting Absolutely Frank any minute now and—

TED: Aha! You *are* Jimmy Fitz!

JAMIE: *(On phone)* This is Jamie . . . Jamie Fitzpatrick.

TED: Whatever. Listen, Jimmy—

JAMIE: *(On phone)* Jamie.

TED: Yeah, right. Aren't ya even gonna guess who this is?

JAMIE: *(On phone)* No.

TED: *(Whining)* Aw, c'mon . . . play.

JAMIE: *(On phone)* Either you tell me who you are right now or I'm hanging up.

TED: Jeez, what a grump. It's me . . . Ted.

JAMIE: *(On phone)* Who?

TED: Ted. Remember? Frank's cousin?

JAMIE: *(On phone—wary)* Oh. Right. I remember you. How'd you get this number?

TED: What's it to ya? Listen, Jimmy—

JAMIE: *(On phone)* Jamie!

TED: Uh huh. Ya see, the thing of it is, Frank won't be in today. As a matter of fact, Frank won't be in for a while. He's after havin' a bit of a accident. He had a argument with a Chevy Blazer and . . . well, he lost. He's in the hospital for a few weeks, and he's in no shape to be fartin' around on the radio.

JAMIE: *(On phone)* Oh. I see. Just how bad is he?

TED: Ah, he'll be all right . . . sooner or later. But, see, the thing of it is . . . he's after catchin' amnesia.

JAMIE: *(On phone)* He's . . . what?

TED: Ya know what it's like . . . ya go in the hospital with one thing wrong, ya come out with another. Well, he caught amnesia in there. He haven't got a clue who he is, where he is, or what he is.

JAMIE: *(On phone)* I didn't know you could catch amnesia.

TED: Oh yeah . . . it's a one-in-a-million chance, and Frank lost. Although, it seems like it's pretty common among politicians. Maybe it's spread by kissin' so much butt . . .

JAMIE: *(On phone)* Look, what exactly do you want, Ted?

TED: Well, now, I figure, with Frank down for the count, so to speak, ya could prob'ly use someone to fill in for him. I figure that someone oughta be . . . me.

JAMIE: *(On phone)* Uh . . . I don't think so.

TED: I don't see why not. We're like two peas in the proverbial pod. We're that close, now, we're practically the same person.

JAMIE: *(On phone)* Didn't we take out a Bond on you? After you got in here and broke some equipment?

TED: Water under the bridge, there, Jimmy.

JAMIE: *(On phone)* Jamie . . .

SOUND: INTERMITTENT BEEPING (CALL WAITING)

TED: Yeah, yeah . . . tomayto, tomahto. Well, whaddya say? Hey, hold on a sec there, Jimmy, I got another call.

JAMIE: *(On phone)* That's Jam—

SOUND: TED SWITCHES TO OTHER LINE.

TED: You've reached the residence of Absolutely Frank. Wait for the beep and then blow it out yer—

HAZEL: *(On phone—terse)* Hello, Ted.

TED: Hazel? Is that you? Where ya callin' from this time?

HAZEL: *(On phone)* Yes, it's me, Ted. And I'm back. I'm at the hospital. What have you done to Frank?

TED: Me? I didn't do nothin' to him. If ya must know, I was just on the phone to CBC, tryin' to save his crappy job for him.

HAZEL: *(On phone)* Don't say another word, Ted. Just listen to me very carefully. You may as well know . . . I'm divorcing Frank.

TED: *Yer what????*

HAZEL: *(On phone)* I suppose my timing could be better, but . . . well, there it is. These last few months flying around the world have enlarged my horizons. I don't intend to spend the rest of my life coddling Frank through his moods, and I definitely don't need to be related to you. I'm a changed woman, Ted. I've discovered the real Hazel at last, and now . . . well, I've just got to be me.

TED: Jeez, Hazel, I never met anyone who's more "you" than you are.

HAZEL: *(On phone)* Don't try to confuse me, Ted. I've made my decision. In the meantime, I've assumed all legal responsibility in Frank's place. I want you out of our house this instant or I'll have you arrested for trespassing. And if there's so much as a doily missing, I'll have you arrested for robbery.

TED: Hey, wait a minute, Hazel. You're not the boss of me . . .

HAZEL: *(On phone)* Shut up, Ted.

TED: I think Frank oughta have some say in this . . .

HAZEL: *(On phone)* Frank is no condition to say anything. Doctor Wu isn't very optimistic about his chances for recovery, and I have to get on with my life.

TED: Doctor Wu??? Hold on there, Hazel, lemme tell ya somethin' about Doctor Wu—

HAZEL: *(On phone)* Goodbye, Ted. Get out of my house.

TED: What about the kids? Where are they?

HAZEL: *(On phone)* None of your business, Ted. Get out.

TED: *(Fading)* What about the CBC?

HAZEL: *(On phone—fading)* I'll deal with the CBC. Get out.

FRANK: *(On phone/in background—fading)* Hazel . . . ? Is that really you, Hazel?

HAZEL: *(On phone—fading)* Frank! You're awake! Oh dear. Brace yourself, Frank—I've got good news and I've got bad news . . .

FRANK: *(On phone/in background—fading)* You mean . . . there's a difference?

July 1996

Hard, Hard Times

Jodean Tobin is Premier Brian Tobin's lovely wife. No disrespect intended!

TED: Boys oh boys . . . what a hellish month this has been. Frank's finally home from the hospital, but he still got amnesia. Hazel still wants to divorce the poor sap. Chuck Furey still won't return my calls. Townies are committin' mass fat-fire suicide, baymen are gone ballistic altogether. And now there's the Mad Fish Disease . . . tsk, tsk, tsk. Things fall apart, the centre cannot hold.

And meantime, what of me? Ah, gentle listener, yer old pal Cousin Ted has fallen on hard times indeed. Hazel got a Court Order to keep me away from her and Frank, and my life has become a vast wasteland. Welfare finally caught on to me and cut me off without a dime. Then Sobey's and Dominion and every corner store downtown put my picture up on their walls, so I'm stuck with the Food Bank, and how many half-blocks of margarine and tins of potted meat can one man stand?

And as if all that wasn't bad enough, I'm not even gettin' any . . . "action," if ya know what I mean. My personal ads in The Telegram produced nothin' but crank calls, the women at my favourite fern bar *are all a buncha hags what I wouldn't be caught dead with,* and my inflatable Jodean Tobin doll got a rip in it. What's a guy to do? I mean, I got powerful needs, if ya catch my drift, and the longer this goes on, the better the chances that I'll end up on a libidinous rampage, a danger to myself and a menace to the community at large.

In the interests of public safety, then, there's only one alternative ... what'd I do with that phone number?

SOUND: TED RUMMAGES THROUGH SOME PAPERS.

TED: Ah! Here we go . . . desperate times call for desperate measures.

SOUND: TED DIALS A PHONE NUMBER.

TED: 1-900-451-8200 . . .

SOUND: PHONE RINGS A FEW TIMES AND IS ANSWERED.

SEDUCTIVE FEMALE VOICE: Hello, this is ... Melissa. This call will cost you $3.33 a minute, with a fifteen minute minimum. How may I help you today?

TED: Well, that's a good question there, Melissa. What're ya doin' right now?

S.F.V.: I'm doing whatever you want me to be doing. May I ask your name?

TED: My name is . . . uh . . . Fred. Yeah, that's right . . . Fred.

S.F.V.: Well then, Fred, what would you like me to be doing?

TED: Ah . . . I'm not sure. What are my choices?

S.F.V.: Fred, your choices are infinite. For the next fifteen minutes, I'm all yours. Are you lying down?

TED: No, actually I'm kinda hunched over at the moment. But I can lie down if I have to. Listen . . . Melissa, right? What're ya wearin'?

S.F.V: I'm naked, Fred. Are you naked?

TED: Well . . . no. But I can be. Is it required?

S.F.V.: Nothing is required, Fred ... except the $3.33 a minute, of course. No, nothing is required ... nothing is impossible, everything is permitted.

TED: Say ... your last name wouldn't happen to be

Nietzsche, would it? Of the Monchy Street Nietzsches?

S.F.V.: There are no last names here, Fred. There is only . . . the moment. Your moment. Or moments, as the case may be.

TED: Ya know, you sound awful familiar. Have we ever met?

S.F.V.: Oh, I don't think so, Fred.

TED: Whaddya look like, Melissa?

S.F.V.: How do you want me to look?

TED: Uh . . . how about tall and blonde? Like Sharon Stone or Tipper Gore, maybe.

S.F.V.: You're in luck, Fred. That's exactly how I look.

TED: Are you sure we've never met? I could swear . . .

S.F.V.: Would you like me to swear, Fred? Would you like me to call you names? Or would you like to call *me* names?

TED: Uh . . . maybe later. Where're ya from, Melissa?

S.F.V.: I'm from the uninhibited Wild Kingdom of your dreams, Fred.

TED: I know I've heard that accent before . . .

S.F.V.: I'm beginning to think your heart isn't in this, Fred. Let's get back on track. I'm naked and I'm perspiring. Hot little beads of moisture are trickling down between my—

TED: *I know that voice! Hazel! What the hell're ya doin'?*

HAZEL: Ted?

TED: Jeez, Hazel . . . does Frank know what you're up to?

HAZEL: *(Horrified)Ted????? (Mortified)* Oh my God . . .

TED: I'd say an explanation is in order here.

HAZEL: I don't need to explain anything to you.

TED: Maybe if I has a few words with Frank . . .

HAZEL: Waste of time, Ted. Frank doesn't even know who *he* is, much less who *I* am.

TED: Well . . . for God's sake, Hazel, what're ya doin' this for?

HAZEL: For money, you twit. I have to make a living somehow. Frank is in cloud-cuckoo land for the time being . . . and even a mediocre divorce lawyer costs a small fortune.

TED: Cripes, Hazel, ya can't divorce Frank in the condition he's in. It's . . . it's inhuman!

HAZEL: I can do whatever I want, Ted. And I wouldn't bandy the word "inhuman" about if I were you, you . . . troglodyte. But I am going to wait until he recovers before I have the papers served on him. Not that it's any of your business. Now goodbye. And don't ever call this number again!

TED: Hey, wait a minute! My fifteen minutes aren't up yet!

HAZEL: Fly to hell, Ted.

TED: Aw, c'mon, be Melissa again, willya? Just fer a coupla more minutes. Listen, I'm naked now . . .

HAZEL: Yuck!

TED: Melissa? Hello?

SOUND: CLICK. DIAL TONE.

September 1996

. . . And Now, the Bad News

HAZEL: *(Pensive)* Oh Frank . . . I wish there were some easy way of saying this. Maybe this isn't the best time for it, what with your amnesia and your various shattered limbs and everything, but then again, there's probably no good time for this sort of thing. *(Pause)* Frank? Can you hear me? Frank?

FRANK: *(Rather vague)* Where am I?

HAZEL: You're home, Frank. You're in your own bed.

FRANK: Really? This is my bed?

HAZEL: Yes.

FRANK: It's really comfy.

HAZEL: We bought it last year, remember?

FRANK: No.

HAZEL: Well, we did. It's a Queen-Size mattress. That's what you wanted.

FRANK: Wow. Are you the Queen?

HAZEL: No, Frank. I'm your wife . . . Hazel.

FRANK: Hmm . . . doesn't ring a bell. *(Pause)* So . . . we're married?

HAZEL: Yes. We've been married for nearly twenty years.

FRANK: Really? Twenty years . . . wow. You're very good looking.

HAZEL: Thank you.

FRANK: Why am I all bandaged up like this?

HAZEL: You had an accident, Frank . . . an automobile accident.

FRANK: Really? So, I own a car?

HAZEL: Not any more.

FRANK: Oh. Too bad. I like cars. I think. *(Pause)* Uh . . . what do I do for a living, Hazel? It *is* Hazel, right?

HAZEL: Yes, Frank.

FRANK: I knew it!

HAZEL: As for what you do ... well, you've done several things, over the years. You drove a cab for a while...

FRANK: I like cars.

HAZEL: ... then you worked as a bartender...

FRANK: I like bars, too.

HAZEL: ... and after that, you went into politics...

FRANK: Really? Did I ever get elected to anything?

HAZEL: No.

FRANK: Thank God.

HAZEL: And then you ended up doing freelance work for CBC Radio.

FRANK: Doing what?

HAZEL: Oh . . . you'd go on the air and complain about the state of the city, the state of the province, the state of the country . . .

FRANK: Imagine that. And we've been married for twenty years?

HAZEL: Yes. That's what I wanted to talk to you about.

FRANK: Are we happily married?

HAZEL: More or less. Sometimes more, sometimes less. Speaking of which—

FRANK: And CBC actually paid me to complain in public?

HAZEL: Yes . . . but you're missing the point, Frank . . .

FRANK: Gee. They must be really nice at CBC. Or else they're nuts . . .

HAZEL: *(Impatient)* Frank! Listen to me!

FRANK: It's . . . Hazel, right?

HAZEL: Frank . . . I want a divorce.

FRANK: Come again?

HAZEL: I want a divorce. I can't take it any more, Frank. The financial uncertainty, the bills piling up, the stress, your loathsome Cousin Ted driving me bonkers . . .

FRANK: Who?

HAZEL: *(Realizing her mistake)* Uh . . . no one. Never mind.

FRANK: I have a cousin named Ted?

HAZEL: No! That was a Freudian slip! I meant to say . . . your Queen-Size bed!

FRANK: I have a Queen-Size bed named Ted?

HAZEL: Damn it, Frank! Don't confuse me! I want a divorce and that's final! You can keep the house if you like, but I want custody of the kids.

FRANK: We have . . . children?

HAZEL: Two. Axel and Donna.

FRANK: I like kids. Don't I?

HAZEL: Actually, no. You've never liked children. I'm not even sure you like your own children.

FRANK: They're so noisy. And they make such a mess.

HAZEL: How would *you* know? *You* never clean up after them.

FRANK: Don't shout at me . . .

HAZEL: I'll shout if I want to! I've been quiet for twenty years and I've had enough! It's the 90s, you twit! I will not be held back by a middle-aged failure like you! I gave you the best twenty years of my life and what have I got to show for it?

FRANK: A Queen-Size bed?

HAZEL: A Queen-Size rage, that's what! And you know something, Frank? It feels good! It feels good to shout at you! I wish I'd shouted at you more often! Maybe if I'd shouted at you more often, you might have done something with your miserable life!

FRANK: It can't be that miserable . . . we have a house and a car and a Queen-Size bed . . .

HAZEL: *Will you shut up about the bloody bed???*

FRANK: Sorry.

HAZEL: As far as I'm concerned, you can stay in that bed until your head falls off!
PAUSE.

FRANK: Gee . . . are all marriages like this?

HAZEL: In 1996? I'd say . . . yes.

FRANK: Wow. What would Statistics Canada have to say about that?

HAZEL: I don't know, Frank. I just know that . . . I want out. *(Pause)* Frank? Did you hear me?
PAUSE.

FRANK: Uh . . . what'd you say your name was?

HAZEL: *Aaaaaggggghhhh!!!!*

September 1996

It Rhymes With Verbose

SOUND: LADDER THUMPS AGAINST SIDE OF HOUSE.

TED: *(Climbing)* Jeez . . . why couldn't ya live in a bungalow, Frank. I haven't clumb up one of these since the old B & E days . . .

SOUND: TED RAPS ON WINDOW PANE.

TED: *(Out of breath)* Hey, Frank! Lemme in, will ya?

SOUND: FRANK OPENS THE WINDOW.

FRANK: What the hell . . . ?

TED: Move outta the way, there, Frank. Jeez, I'm beat to a snot. I couldn't bust two strands of a drool.

FRANK: Who are you and what do you want?

TED: It's me, Frank—Ted. Your cousin? Ya know? Lemme in out of it, now. I don't like heights, and heights don't like me.

SOUND: TED CLIMBS IN AND FALLS ON THE FLOOR.

TED: Ouch!

FRANK: Are you all right?

TED: Yeah, yeah, I'm fine. Number One. Listen, is Hazel home? She'll peel me if she catches me up here.

FRANK: Who?

TED: Hazel, Frank . . . yer wife?

FRANK: Well . . . there's some woman who *says* she's my wife, but . . .

TED: Ya still got the amnesia, have ya?

FRANK: I guess so.

TED: We'll see about that. Ya sure you don't know who I am?

FRANK: I know who you say you are . . . my Cousin Ted. Right?

TED: Right. Now, what's my middle name?

FRANK: I don't know.

TED: Sure ya do. Ya used to be on my case about it all the time when we were kids. *(Pause)* Well? *(Pause)* I'll give ya a hint—it rhymes with Aloysius.

FRANK: Nothing rhymes with Aloysius.

TED: G'wan, boy, give it a shot.

FRANK: Well . . . okay. Delicious?

TED: No.

FRANK: Suspicious?

TED: No.

FRANK: Fictitious?

TED: That's not funny, Frank.

FRANK: Oh for God's sake . . . I give up. What is it?

TED: Yer useless, Frank . . . all right, it's Ignatius.

FRANK: Ignatius!? That doesn't rhyme with Aloysius.

TED: It don't?

FRANK: Besides, your middle name isn't Ignatius . . . it's Ambrose.

TED: Aha! Gotcha! You're fakin', buddy! I knew it!

FRANK: All right, all right. I haven't got amnesia. Happy now? Just don't tell Hazel.

TED: Don't worry, Frank. Ya can trust the old Ted-man. We're blood. *(Pause)* Ya mind tellin' me what you're up to?

FRANK: Oh come on, you know perfectly well what I'm up to.

TED: Ya mean . . . the d-i-v-o-r-s-e?

FRANK: Well, the longer I have amnesia, the longer she'll put it off. And the longer she puts it off, the more likely she is to change her mind.

TED: Change her mind!? Jeez, Frank . . . listen, buddy, ya'd be better off without her. You got no idea what she's doin' to make a few bucks on the side...

SOUND DOOR OPENS.

HAZEL: Good Lord!!! How did you ... ? Get out of here right now!

TED: Well, well, well ... if it isn't "Melissa" the party girl, in person.

HAZEL: Out! Out! Out!

TED: I'm goin', I'm goin' ...

SOUND: TED CLIMBS BACK OUT THE WINDOW.

HAZEL: And put that ladder back in the shed!

TED: I'll call ya later, "Melissa" ... 1-900-451 -

SOUND: HAZEL SLAMS THE WINDOW.

TED: *(Falling)* Aaaaaagggggghhhhhh!

SOUND: TED LANDS IN THE SHRUBBERY.

TED: *(From a distance)* Ow! Ow! Ow!

FRANK: Who was that?

HAZEL: Hmm? Oh ... obviously some deluded derelict with a severe personality disorder. Forget about him, Frank.

FRANK: He called you Melissa. I thought you said your name was Hazel.

HAZEL: It is.

FRANK: *(Fading)* Then why did he call you Melissa?

HAZEL: *(Fading)* No, no, he called me "Missus." You just *thought* he said "Melissa." You're confused, Frank. Try not to think about it.

FRANK: *(Fading)* I'm pretty sure he called you Melissa ...

HAZEL: *(Fading)* It was *Missus*, I tell you! *Missus! Missus!*

October 1996

Talking Turkey

SOUND: FRANK MUNCHES ON A TURKEY SANDWICH.

FRANK: *(With mouth full)* Mmm . . . this is one helluva good turkey sandwich. Yummy.

HAZEL: Step away from the sandwich, Frank. We have to talk.

FRANK: *(Still munching)* Are we gonna talk turkey? *(Pause)* Get it? "Turkey sandwich"—"talk turkey?" *(Pause)* That's a joke.

HAZEL: Focus, Frank. We really need to have a serious talk.

FRANK: *(Wary)* Well . . . okay. What do you want to talk about?

HAZEL: About us, Frank.

FRANK: What about us?

HAZEL: You know as well as I do that we have some serious problems to work out.

FRANK: We do?

HAZEL: Yes.

FRANK: Well, y'know, with this amnesia and everything, I really don't remember much of anything before the car accident.

HAZEL: Frank, enough is enough—I don't think you have amnesia at all.

FRANK: You don't?

HAZEL: I know you, Frank. I think you're pretending to have amnesia so you won't have to face reality.

FRANK: I think "reality" is one of those words that should always have quotes around it. Like "democracy" or "national identity" or . . .

HAZEL: You're evading the issue again, Frank. That's what you always do. Whenever you don't want to deal with something unpleasant, you change the subject. You pretend you don't know what I'm talking about, or that you have amnesia or a brain tumor or something.

FRANK: Maybe I do have a brain tumor. I know I've got one giant jackhammer of a headache . . .

HAZEL: Let's see if we can jog your memory. You know who I am, don't you?

FRANK: Yes. You're my wife Hazel and we've been married for twenty years. Or so you tell me.

HAZEL: Do you remember how we met?

FRANK: Uh . . . skating at the stadium?

HAZEL: No. Here's a hint—your Cousin Ted's parole hearing.

FRANK: Which one?

HAZEL: It was right after all the downtown bars burned down.

FRANK: Was Ted a suspect?

HAZEL: Ted is *always* a suspect. Anyway, don't you remember me asking you out for coffee afterwards?

FRANK: Hmm . . . coffee . . . y'know, a cup of coffee'd go down good with this sandwich . . .

HAZEL: Forget the sandwich, Frank. Pay attention. Do you remember our wedding?

FRANK: We didn't go over Churchill Falls in a barrel or anything, did we? I have this vague memory of falling and being really wet . . .

HAZEL: Yes! We were married at Bannerman Park and Ted pushed you into the pool! Remember that?

FRANK: No, it was Bowring Park and *you* pushed me—oops.

HAZEL: Hmph. So much for the amnesia.

FRANK: *(Evasive)* Victoria Park? Pippy Park? Bally Haly?

HAZEL: Stop it, Frank.

PAUSE.

FRANK: Butterpot Park?

HAZEL: *(Warning)* Frank . . .

FRANK: Oh, all right . . . yes, I've been faking the amnesia.

HAZEL: But why, Frank? Why?

FRANK: Because you're right, Hazel. I can't deal with any of this anymore. With politicians or the economy or Labrador separatism or CBC cutbacks or Ted or you . . . It's easier if I just pretend I haven't got a clue about what's going on. I'd make a perfect Cabinet Minister, don't you think?

HAZEL: Nice try, Frank, but you're not changing *this* subject. I'm telling you for the last time, we either do something about this marriage or . . . we pack it in.

FRANK: Pack it in?

HAZEL: People get divorced all the time, Frank. It's messy, but it's not the end of the world.

FRANK: Please don't say the "D" word, Hazel. I can't take it. I can't live, if living is without you. I can't live, I can't give anymore . . .

HAZEL: Don't quote old song lyrics at me, Frank. I hate it when you do that.

FRANK: Okay, I'll never do it again. I'll do anything you want, Hazel. Or I *won't* do anything you *don't* want me to do. Whatever you say. Just don't . . . please, can't we start over? I'll change, I swear I will. I'll talk about my "feelings," I'll be more "sensitive"...

HAZEL: You're putting quotes around those words, Frank.

FRANK: Sorry. Habit.

HAZEL: I just want you to be more open with me, Frank. You used to be open with me. You used to tell me everything. What happened? What changed you?

FRANK: I think it was . . . "reality."

HAZEL: You're doing it again.

FRANK: Sorry. But look around, Hazel. Look at Newfoundland. Look at us. Everything is going down the drain, and I feel like we're going with it.

HAZEL: You're just depressed, Frank. It's really not that bad. Things will get better.

FRANK: They will if you'll reconsider the div—the "D" word. Will you? Hmm?

PAUSE.

HAZEL: Yes, Frank. Yes, I will. Yes.

FRANK: *(Relieved)* Whew. Y'know, I feel better already. I see better days ahead, a brighter tomorrow, our full and fair share . . .

HAZEL: Don't push it, Frank. Just finish your sandwich for now. Let's just take it one step at a time, shall we?

SOUND: (FADING) FRANK EATS HIS TURKEY SANDWICH.

FRANK: *(Fading—chewing & singing)* "Happy days are here again, the skies above are clear again . . . "

October 1996

Mr. Melonhead Has a Plan . . . A *Big* Plan

Margaret Dunn is a well-known St John's cosmetologist. "The Rock of the Rock" is the on-air nickname of a cheesy local radio station, OZ-FM. The "Splash-and-Putt" is . . . the "Splash-and-Putt." The voice of the grocery store clerk was provided by CBC Production Secretary Chloe Budgell.

SOUND: GENERAL SUPERMARKET SOUNDS (ROLLING SHOPPING CARTS, SUBDUED MUZAK, THE FAINT "PING!" OF ELECTRONIC CASH REGISTERS, ETC.) ESTABLISH AND CONTINUE UNDER.

FRANK: Hmm . . . let's see . . . have I got everything? Better check my list again. Kitty litter for Fluffy . . . yes. Purity Jam-Jams for me . . . yes. Some of that Marmite goo Hazel likes on her toast . . . yes. Wieners and marshmallows for Bonfire Night . . . yes. And maybe one of these nice juicy cantaloupes . . .

TED: Ow! Stop squeezin' my head, Frank.

FRANK: Ted!? What the hell . . . ? I thought you were a cantaloupe.

TED: Well, I'm not. I'm a honeydew melon.

FRANK: What are you doing here? I thought you were barred-for-life from every grocery store in town.

TED: They can't bar me if they can't see me. That's why I'm disguised as produce.

FRANK: Very effective, Ted. But . . . you look like more like a cantaloupe than a honeydew.

TED: Blame it on that shaggin' "Animal, Vegetable or

Mineral Make-Up Course" I took from Margaret Dunn. Money down the drain, Frank.

FRANK: You haven't answered my question. What are you doing here?

TED: It's the only way I can get to see ya. Hazel changed all the locks on yer house, and she got Fluffy trained to scrob the face off me if I even pokes my head over the back yard fence.

FRANK: Fluffy does that to everyone. She does it to *me.*

TED: When I think of all the time I wasted tryin' to establish a mental link with that stinkin' cat . . . anyway, listen, Frank, I gotta ask ya somethin'. I'm hearin' some ugly rumours . . . rumours about you and Hazel . . . rumours about you and the CBC . . .

FRANK: They're not rumours, Ted. Hazel called off the divorce and we're going to renew our wedding vows. We might even go on a second honeymoon.

TED: Oh yeah? Where to this time? Karwood Kabins again?

FRANK: We're going *alone* this time, Ted. We're thinking maybe the Splash-and-Putt . . .

TED: Jeez, Frank, I . . . I don't know what to say. I'm stunned.

FRANK: Uh huh. Anyway, it's time for me and Hazel to move on, and that's exactly what we're going to do. I suggest you do the same. It's time for some big changes.

TED: Uh oh. I don't like the sound of this, Frank. What about you and the CBC?

FRANK: Well, CBC is going through some big changes, too. We've all got to make adjustments. I'm thinking about giving the whole thing up, to tell you the truth. I want to try something new.

TED: Ya don't mean . . . yer goin' over to the Rock of the Rock? Say it ain't so, Frank!

FRANK:	Jesus, no. I'm not crazy.
CLERK:	'Scuse me, mister. Are you gonna buy that cantaloupe or are ya just gonna talk to it? 'Cause we got a strict policy about talkin' to the produce, y'know.
FRANK:	Uh . . . no. It looks a bit over-ripe. I'll just check out my groceries and go home. Goodbye, Ted.
TED:	Frank! Wait! Ya can't do this! If ya go off the air, where does that leave me? *You'll* be makin' whoopee at the Splash-and-Putt and *I'll* be twistin' in the wind!
CLERK:	Shut up, fruit.
TED:	Yer forcin' me to take drastic action, Frank! Don't make me do somethin' desperate!
FRANK:	You're crouching in a fruit bin, pretending to be a melon. How much more desperate can you get?
TED:	Frank! Come back!
CLERK:	Hey! I knows you—you're not a cantaloupe! You're Ted! I'm callin' the manager . . .
TED:	Stop squeezin' my head, Missus!
CLERK:	Help! This cantaloupe bit me!
TED:	*(Fading)* Frank! This isn't over, buddy! I will not be ignored! I got a plan . . . a *big* plan! Ya haven't heard the last of me!
MUSIC:	"DRAGNET" THEME (1st Riff).
TED:	*(Fading)* I said leggo my head!
MUSIC:	"DRAGNET" THEME (2nd Riff)

November 1996

Top of the World, Ma!

This was the last "Absolutely Frank" that I recorded for Week-End A.M. My thanks to all the CBC folks who agreed to help out—Regional Director Ron Crocker, Executive Producer Anne Budgell, Executive Producer Glen Tilley, Producer Ingrid Fraser, Producer Jamie Fitzpatrick, Associate Producer Suzanne Woolridge, Announcer Richard Beaton, and of course, Producer Francesca Swann, who provided the Voice of Hazel for me for so long.

I was going to go with "Ending Number One" until Ingrid suggested doing both endings. This was a perfect opportunity for me to finally pay homage to The Goon Show *(Peter Sellers, Spike Milligan & Harry Secombe—BBC Radio, 1951-1960), which had been a major inspiration for my own sense of humour.*

God bless you, one and all.

SOUND: STUDIO DOOR OPENS AND CLOSES.

FRANK: Well, here it is, Hazel—good ol' Studio "A."

HAZEL: *(Unimpressed)* Very nice, Frank.

FRANK: Yes, I've had a lot of good times up here. I'm gonna miss the ol' place. Look, here's my favourite headset . . . and this is the microphone I always use. Good ol' microphone . . .

SOUND: STUDIO DOOR OPENS. INGRID ENTERS.

INGRID: Frank? You're a little early, aren't you?

FRANK: Ingrid! Hi! Come in, I want you to meet someone. Hazel, this is my producer, Ingrid. Ingrid . . . my wife, Hazel.

INGRID: Well, this is a pleasure, Hazel. I thought you were just a figment of Frank's imagination. So . . . what's it going to be today, Frank? Any bizarre sound effects or weird music?

FRANK: No, it's very simple, Ingrid. Just a little mood piece about Autumn and Winter. *(Wistful)* You know, endings and beginnings, that sort of thing. It's kind of . . . poetic.

INGRID: Whatever. Let me just wake up a technician, and we'll —

SOUND: STUDIO DOOR CLOSES. TED ENTERS.

TED: Stay right where ya are! Don't nobody move!

FRANK: Ted? What now?

TED: I warned ya I'd do somethin' drastic, Frank.

FRANK: What are you talking about?

TED: I want everybody in this building *in* here right now!

FRANK: Don't be ridiculous, Ted. They'd never fit.

TED: Well then . . . all the Week-End A.M. people. Get 'em all up here—or else.

FRANK: Or else what?

TED: Never mind. Just get 'em. You—whassyer name—Ingrid. Get on the horn, toot sweet.

HAZEL: What've you got under your coat, Ted?

TED: Take a good look, Hazel. I'm wired to blow!

INGRID: My God, that looks like . . .

TED: That's right, Missus—I'm wrapped from head to toe with C-4 plastic explosive!

HAZEL: Ted! Have you gone completely mad?

TED: That's fer me to know and you to find out. I wants hostages! Lots of 'em! Then I wants free air time to read my list of demands!

FRANK: Demands!? What demands?

TED: *(Sotto voce)* Just play along with me, Frank—I'll have yer job back for ya in no time.

FRANK: I don't want my job back, Ted. I told you—it's time to move on.

TED: Too late, Frank. The die is cast. C'mon, there, Ingrid—get those people up here! Or I'll blow us all to Merasheen right now!

FRANK: Better do as he says, Ingrid.

INGRID: *(On phone—nervous)* Could I have everyone in the Week-End A. M. office up in Studio "A" right away? We've got a, uh . . . a situation here.

TED: That's a nice little hat yer wearin' there, Ingrid.

INGRID: Take it! It's yours! Just let me out of here! I have a child!

TED: That's what they all say.

SOUND: STUDIO DOOR OPENS AS ANNE, RON, JAMIE GLEN AND SUZANNE ENTER. DOOR CLOSES.

ANNE: *(Steamed)* This had better be important, Ingrid. I was right in the middle of a meeting with Ron and Glen.

FRANK: Anne . . . Ron . . . Jamie . . . Glen . . . Suzanne . . . meet my Cousin Ted.

JAMIE: Oh Jesus, not you again! Someone call the cops!

TED: Pipe down, Jimmy.

JAMIE: *(Exasperated)* That's Jamie.

TED: Whatever. Which one of ya is Ron Crocker?

RON: Uh . . . that would be me.

GLEN: *(Sarcastic)* Good move, Ron. Now he knows what you look like. Why don't you give him your phone number while you're at it?

TED: Who the hell're you?

GLEN: Glen Tilley.

TED: Jeez, it's amazin' what make-up can do. Ya don't look anythin' like ya do on TV.

GLEN: *(Sighs)* Not you, too? That's the other Glen Tilley...

ANNE: Come on, Ron—talk to this nut! Show some leadership!

RON: Stop pushing me! Uh . . . look here . . . Ted, is it? What exactly do you want?

TED: What do I want? What do I want? I wants . . . uh . . . I wants a lifetime contract fer my favourite cousin, Frank.

RON: Not a friggin' chance.

TED: Well, then—shag Frank. I wants my own show—"The Wonderful World of Ted"—every midnight.

RON: No can do.

TED: Jeez, yer one tough negotiator, all right—how about if I settles fer a cup of coffee and a muffin?

SUZANNE: Sorry—no coffee, no muffins. Budget cutbacks.

TED: That's it! That's the last straw! I'm mad as hell and I'm not gonna take it anymore! If there's no Frank and no muffins, then there won't be no CBC! We're goin' up in smoke and we're all goin' together! I'm pullin' the pin!

ALL: No!!!!

TED: Top of the world, Frank! Top of the world! Here goes!

HAZEL: I love you, Frank!

SOUND: THE INEFFECTUAL SQUIRT OF A DAMP SQUIB. PAUSE.

TED: Had ya goin' there, didn't I?

HAZEL: Damn you, Ted . . .

FRANK: Let me see that stuff . . . that's not C-4. It's . . . it's Silly Putty!

TED: I tried my best for ya, Frank, but I'm not nuts, y'know.

RON: Ted—you're fired.

TED: Ya can't fire me, Crocker! I don't work here!

RON: All right, everyone. Back to work. Chop-chop. Oh, and Frank—*you're* fired.

FRANK: *(Fading)* This is my last day, Ron—you *can't* fire me.

RON: *(Fading)* Aw, come on—let me fire *someone*.

TED: *(Fading)* Hey! What am I gonna do with all this friggin' Silly Putty?

PAUSE.

RICHARD BEATON: That was "Ending Number One." And now, here's "Ending Number Two."

SUZANNE: Sorry—no coffee, no muffins. Budget cutbacks.

TED: That's it! That's the last straw! I'm mad as hell and I'm not gonna take it anymore! If there's no Frank and no muffins, then there won't be no CBC! We're goin' up in smoke and we're all goin' together!

RON: Ted—you're fired.

TED: Ya can't fire me, Crocker! I don't work here!

RON: I can fire anyone I want to.

TED: Ya can't stop me, buddy! I'm pullin' the pin!

ALL: No!!!

TED: Top of the world, Frank! Top of the world! Here goes!

HAZEL: I love you, Frank!

SOUND: THE BIGGEST, LOUDEST, LONGEST EXPLOSION IN THE SOUND EFFECTS LIBRARY.

PAUSE.

RICHARD BEATON: And that, dear listeners, is why the CBC Radio Building you see on Duckworth Street is really only a cardboard replica . . .

TED: *(Far in the distance — full reverb — as he is blown into the stratosphere)* Tttoooppp ooofff ttthhheee wwwooorrrlllddd, FFFrrraaannnkkk . . . .

November 1996